Passionate Supervision

by the same editor

Passionate Medicine
Making the Transition from Conventional Medicine to Homeopathy
Edited by Robin Shohet
ISBN 978 1 84310 298 4

of related interest

Good Practice in Supervision
Statutory and Voluntary Organisations
Edited by Jacki Pritchard
ISBN 978 1 85302 279 1

Integrative Approaches to Supervision
Edited by Michael Carroll and Margaret Tholstrup
ISBN 978 1 85302 966 0

Creative Supervision
The Use of Expressive Arts Methods in Supervision and
Self-Supervision
Mooli Lahad
ISBN 978 1 85302 828 1

Relating to Clients
The Therapeutic Relationship for Complementary Therapists
Su Fox
ISBN 978 1 84310 615 9

Counsellors in Health Settings
Edited by Kim Etherington
Foreword by Tim Bond
ISBN 978 1 85302 938 7

Working Ethics
How to Be Fair in a Culturally Complex World
Richard Rowson
ISBN 978 1 85302 750 5

Spirituality, Ethics and Care
Simon Robinson
ISBN 978 1 84310 498 8

Passionate Supervision

Edited by Robin Shohet

Jessica Kingsley Publishers
London and Philadelphia

First published in 2008
by Jessica Kingsley Publishers
116 Pentonville Road
London N1 9JB, UK
and
400 Market Street, Suite 400
Philadelphia, PA 19106, USA

www.jkp.com

Library of Congress Cataloging in Publication Data
Passionate supervision / edited by Robin Shohet.
    p. cm.
Includes index.
ISBN 978-1-84310-556-5 (pbk. : alk. paper) 1. Counselors–Supervision of. 2.
Psychotherapists–Supervision of. 3. Social workers–Supervision of. I. Shohet, Robin.
BF637.C6P37 2008
361.0068'3–dc22

British Library Cataloguing in Publication Data
A CIP catalogue record for this book is available from the British Library

ISBN 978 1 84310 556 5

Printed and bound in Great Britain by
MPG Books Limited, Cornwall

To Angeline and Sammy

Acknowledgements

First and foremost I would like to thank my colleagues and friends from the Centre for Supervision and Team Development, Peter Hawkins, Judy Ryde and my partner Joan Wilmot. We have worked and played together for 30 years, and most of what I know about supervision, I have learnt with and through you.

Second, I would like to appreciate all the contributors to this book. You all turned up for an authors' meeting just before Christmas from all parts of England, Wales and Scotland and even from Greece, and many of you have attended subsequent meetings which I greatly appreciate. I have felt that you have willingly supported the project far more than just writing your individual chapters.

Third, I would like to acknowledge the Course in Miracles on my thinking. Even after studying it for many years, I still feel like a beginner and grapple with living its central theme of moving from fear to love. Related to this I would like to thank all those who have attended my workshops on fear and love in supervision whose contributions inspired me to write my chapter.

Finally I would like to thank Jessica Kingsley Publishers for publishing *Passionate Medicine* which led to the idea of a book on *Passionate Supervision*.

Contents

Foreword

Woody Allen once said that 95 per cent of success was turning up. When I first heard this I laughed and thought 'That is easy, all I need to do is to arrive at the right place at the right time and I will be a success'. If only it were that easy! To really turn up for work means to bring all of yourself into work, not just part of your brain, but your full emotional, sensing, relating, reflecting, experiencing being and not just turning up physically but having your mind, body and spirit all engaged with what needs to be done. The next time you are about to start a supervision session, I would invite you to stop and pause and check how much of you has turned up for this session. How much of you is fully awake and present – not focused on the past, worrying about the unfinished items on your action list or planning your next weekend away, but fully in the now, ready to receive whatever may emerge or surprise you in the coming encounter?

To learn to be fully present is a lifetime endeavour and work provides us with one of the major classrooms for this learning. Arguably the most important gift of the supervisor to their supervisee is to role model full presence (Senge *et al.* 2005). But this book encourages each of us to go beyond being fully present to finding the passion. For many of these writers passion is similar to Henri Bergson's 'Elan Vital' or spirit of life. They show how it encompasses a spirit of inquiry, a love of learning, an openness to others, a difference which is free from preconceptions and fixed opinions and a generosity that can share one's own experience without knowing better or knowing first. Robin Shohet ends the book with a chapter showing how, if we are to find the passion in our work, we have to constantly overcome our fear – the fear of getting it wrong, of not knowing, of otherness – to allow our love for life to fully flow.

We each spend a great deal of our lives at work. For some, work is merely a necessity to finance the rest of what matters to them – their family, their hobbies, their holidays. So often this is a recipe for work becoming soulless and en route to drudgery. To lead a full life is to find work we can love and work that is a source of constant learning and development of our potential. Freud wrote that health is about the ability to love and to work, and the archetypal psychologist James Hillman (1983) commented that since Freud's time so much more time has been spent exploring the area of love than has been spent on how to love one's work.

This book brings together a wide range of writers from different professions, all of whom clearly not only love their work but have a passion to share their experience and inspire others to engage more fully in their work relationships. In *Supervision in the Helping Professions* (Hawkins and Shohet 2006) we wrote about how supervision can easily be reduced to this qualitative function, that is, ensuring the quality of the work with the clients and ignoring the educative and supportive functions. The educative or developmental function itself can be reduced to senior practitioners inducting more junior practitioners into the skills and ways of operating currently used in the profession. It thus becomes a top down enculturation process with the supervisor supposedly having the 'super vision' which they can impart to the supervisee.

I believe that supervision is not done by the supervisor, but rather jointly by the supervisor and supervisee together. By attending to the work with clients in a spirit of open inquiry both the supervisor and the supervisee should be learning, and through them so should the profession. When we first started writing about supervision in the early 1980s, supervision was mainly limited to the fields of mental health. Over the last 20 years we have witnessed a phenomenal spread of supervision right across the helping professions into areas like education, general medicine and alternative health, and this book includes chapters from practitioners in these fields. More recently supervision has also been taken up in the wider 'people professions' in the commercial world with the growth of supervision of executive coaches, organizational consultants and human resources managers. Supervision used to be centred on those who were still in training. Now it is much more recognized that supervision is for life not just for trainees. In the 'people professions', when you stop learning, you stop being effective.

This is a book that unashamedly brings love, spirit and soul into the heart of the supervision process but does so without becoming sanctimonious or precious. We see this through the various heart-felt experiences and stories of the different helping professionals that Robin Shohet has brought together. As the youngest of the supervisors who contribute to this book, Joe Wilmot shows the starting place of becoming a passionate supervisor is not lofty ideals, but to find yourself a good down to earth supervisor and to be honest about what is going on for you. So I hope you enjoy reading these stories and reflections as much as I did and that they encourage you to find, not only love and hope in the midst of the joy of human relationships, but also in the darkness of human sorrows and suffering.

Peter Hawkins, Summer 2007

References

Hawkins, P. and Shohet, R. (2006) *Supervision in the Helping Professions*. Third Edition. Maidenhead: Open University Press McGraw Hill.

Hillman, J. (1983) *Inter Views: Conversations between James Hillman and Laura Pozzo on Therapy, Biography, Love, Soul, Dream, Work, Imagination and the State of Culture*. New York: Harper: Harper & Row.

Senge, P., Otto Scharmer, C., Jaworski, J. and Flowers, B.S. (2005) *Presence: An Explanation of Profound Change in People, Organizations, and Society*. New York: Currency/Doubleday.

Introduction

In the last 20 years supervision has increasingly been seen as a vital part of the repertoire for most of the helping professions – be they doctors, nurses, probation officers, occupational therapists, social workers, counsellors, psychotherapists or related fields. At its best it provides a place to bring issues from work in a safe, but challenging context on the basis that, if carers do not take care of themselves, their client group will suffer from the stresses that are an almost inevitable part of their work.

In this modern world where pressures to act decisively conflict with a fear of being blamed, supervision can provide a much needed time to reflect. I personally think that all workers, not just those in the helping professions, would benefit from this space. In the business world, coaching has become increasingly popular, and in the teaching profession, mentoring. This is not the place to go into the differences, but suffice to say that what supervision, coaching and mentoring have in common is a desire to improve practice through some kind of reflection. They offer an opportunity for us to keep growing, to feel listened to and understood, and challenged when we discover, as we must, our blind spots. Even those who have been practising for a very long time still need recourse to supervision. There is a recognition that we are always on the journey; there is never a time when we have arrived if that means being totally sure of ourselves in every context. In fact one of the marks of a good practitioner is their ability to tolerate uncertainty, not knowing, which can make us feel quite vulnerable. It is the sign of a good supervisory relationship when both parties can co-create an environment where they continue to be open to, and learning from, each other.

The contributors to this book share a passion for supervision and the importance of the supervisory relationship. They are drawn from a variety of the helping professions – creative therapy, psychotherapy, homeopathy, education, youth work. At the beginning of each chapter, I have asked each contributor to say what they most wanted the reader to know and also to give a synopsis. The intention is to help focus both the writer and the reader on the journey they are making together. The thread that runs through all the chapters is asking us to see the world of our clients, supervisees, ourselves and the organizations we might work for with fresh eyes, not allowing ourselves to become myopic with others' expectations. In doing this, the spiritual dimension of the work is often there, sometimes explicitly, sometimes implicitly.

A modern spiritual teacher has written:

> Although you can't find the truth in a book, books are sometimes the way we connect dots in our heads and in our hearts. Sometimes books can open us up in really significant ways. (Adyashanti 2006, p.193)

As editor, my wish is that as you read each chapter you connect the dots in your minds and hearts, allowing them to trigger your own internal supervisor.

Reference

Adyashanti (2006) *Emptiness Dancing*. Boulder, CO: Sounds True.

Introduction to Chapter 1

I knew of Jochen's work with refugees and asylum seekers in the Medical Foundation for the Care of Victims of Torture and saw how it had transformed his practice as a therapist and supervisor. In this chapter we are asked to re-examine many of our beliefs and concepts, our stories of who we think we are. In urging us to think outside our boxes, he is offering a way of listening to ourselves, our supervisees and our clients that is potentially both challenging and liberating.

I asked Jochen what he most wanted the reader to take away from his writing and he replied:

> Writing this chapter has been a challenging, exciting and rather unpredictable journey. It rattled me more than I had expected, pushed me over more edges than I had anticipated and led to insights deeper and more reassuring than I could have ever wished for.
>
> I hope this chapter does for the reader what it has done for me.

Chapter 1

Breaking the Box: Supervision – A Challenge to Free Ourselves

Jochen Encke

A child is having a terrible nightmare.

Isn't our instinct to take it gently in our arms, hold it tenderly and by lovingly talking to it encourage it to wake up?

In this chapter I show how I invite my supervisees to do exactly the same with their clients: rather than to examine their clients' stories and to explore their feelings, I encourage my supervisees to wake up to a bigger reality and, by doing so, help their clients go beyond their own stories. We do not suffer because life is so painful. We suffer because the box we have built around ourselves has become too small. What is needed is not the healing of wounds, but our willingness to break out of our boxes. Passionate supervision offers a way to do this.

I remember my first psychotherapy session many years ago. I was deeply distressed, and I felt pretty hopeless; nothing seemed to work out in my life. For about half an hour I poured out my pain and confusion. I plunged it all in front of my therapist hoping for an analysis and a suggestion how to go about solving these numerous problems.

However, what I received was one sentence delivered in a warm and understanding manner:

My God, Jochen, you are in a pickle!

This sentence threw me. It did not throw me because it would so powerfully help to understand my problems and solve them (because it did not). It was not my mind that got affected. At that time I could not really put words to what had touched me so much. I only could feel a physical response: I observed my stomach muscles relaxing and my diaphragm softly vibrating. A peace started engulfing me from within that I had never experienced before, slowly crawling through my entire body. I had touched a place far deeper than my stories; I had touched what later I would call my soul. An inner smile of recognition appeared from nowhere and if I had allowed it to develop I would most probably have laughed my head off.

Maybe for the first time in my life I had an opportunity to step outside my self-created box – and I did not dare to take it. Instead I stifled that smile! This experience has become the cornerstone for my personal and professional life as a psychotherapist and supervisor, not just because of the smile I had felt so unexpectedly, but also because of my determined effort to stifle it. I pushed it away, because it did not fit into my concept of my self as a suffering and confused young man. Then and there I decided to stick to what I felt familiar and my mind could identify with: 'the story of me as I knew it'. I decided to stay in my box.

Many years I spent trying to understand the 'story of me', 'polishing' my box from inside – and with that making sure I stayed inside. However, I had never forgotten the smile. Often without me noticing it, I was pursuing it.

From time to time I met somebody who reminded me that there is life outside my box. These men and women were like a good parent listening to the sorrow of the child, knowing that what seems so difficult and overwhelming in the child's eyes, actually loses its power when viewed from a wider perspective. They were holding a bigger picture, without denying the reality of my experience. They were seeing something I could not see yet. They were seeing my soul, while I insisted on clinging to my stories.

Then a time came when I recognized my own stories and those of others to be what they really are: just stories. Stories are like boxes we build around ourselves to give us structure, identity, security, and familiarity. We are attached to them even when they are traumatic and painful, because they feel so much part of us. Although breaking the box open would give an immense freedom, the resistance is great since outside that box we feel unprotected and so different to who we believe we are, that we desperately keep it intact. However, stories also limit us; if we grow too big they suffocate us, or if the stories grow too big they squash us and prevent us from being who we really are.

Recognizing that we continuously create and repeat stories is an important step toward breaking our boxes. The process of breaking our boxes, however, then only begins. It becomes a never ending process in which more and more of life's events can be appreciated and seen as merely stories unfolding without needing to get drawn into them. The less we get taken over by stories the more a space opens from which we radiate an immense amount of peace, love and inner strength.

Supervisees come to us with powerful stories to tell from their clients. Whether the supervisee is a medical professional, a social worker or a psychotherapist, what every single practitioner in the helping profession has to deal with is a continuous need of clients and patients to be made to feel better. Something is broken, which needs fixing. Something has gone wrong, which needs being put right. Practitioners can easily get drawn into the presented story, the presented problems, feelings and worries – and with that, stay in the box clients have created for themselves. The more powerful the story and the more painful the feelings, the stronger the box and the more difficult to see anything else.

(I am not suggesting that boxes are all bad. They are there to hold, contain and give a sense of familiarity – at least for a time. Sometimes they even need to be rebuilt when they got shattered too early or too brutally. However, ultimately I suggest even a 'shattered box' is also another story that wants to be left behind.)

Sometimes therapists, social workers, or any other person in the helping profession find themselves in a place of helplessness and hopelessness triggered by powerful stories – maybe a bit similar to that of the medical professional when facing the terminally ill. What do I say to the terminally ill person who knows he will die soon? Words of comfort cannot come any more from the place of hope, the hope that soon things will be better and back to normal. (David Owen has written more about this in Chapter 3.)

When arriving at a place where 'there is nowhere else to go' and accepting it, at that moment life becomes more than just a life that needs fixing. Healing becomes more than saving a body. True support comes from knowing that even 'being terminally ill' is just another story – a powerful one, though. True support comes from knowing that there is more to life than what I experience inside my box.

Obviously it is essential to appreciate the presented story, to deal with the problems, whether it is providing medicine, listening to important life experiences or helping to solve housing or financial problems, etc. Stories are there to be told and listened to. Life is full of them; life is one big story. Stories can be very difficult to bear; they also can be rich, captivating and entertaining. I do not at all want to diminish the importance of stories. Life without stories would be very dull. Stories can be horrible, beautiful and challenging – and they can open doors.

When supervision provides a space in which stories and problems are seen as a gateway to a new dimension of reality, rather than merely as issues which need solving, for me at that moment it becomes 'passionate supervision'.

I call it passionate supervision because I believe passion is the essential ingredient to breaking through intellectual and emotional resistance. Passion as I see it is not a feeling; it is a force capable of deeply affecting others in a subtle and profound way. Any action, any thought or feeling when fed by passion has a hugely transformative power. Passion is not fanatical. Passion is not noisy. Passion is gentle and patient while at the same time fierce and determined. Passion arises when the essence of one's life has been touched and one starts dealing with the world from that place. For me passionate supervision has become this essence. This work has taken me over and has infiltrated my whole being. It is not something I only earn my living with; it is something that occupies every second of my life.

Let me continue with an analogy. Going beyond the stories is a bit similar to seeing a 3-dimensional picture.

At first glance you only see a flat 2-dimensional picture or a large amount of dots in different colours, until you re-adjust your eyes and suddenly a very clear 3-dimensional image appears where the 2-dimensional picture or meaningless and randomly displayed dots had been. It is by looking through the dots and softening your vision, by basically disregarding the 2-dimensional picture, that you discover the new dimension. It is essential for somebody to be there who knows and passionately insists there is more to that 2-dimensional picture and can show you the different way of looking; to find it you have to do it by yourself. Once you know how to re-adjust your eyes it becomes as real as the 2-dimensional picture. It is wonderful and rewarding to watch the faces of those who suddenly for the first time can see this new dimension.

Similarly, first you look at life filled with your stories seemingly happening at random without any reasons or connections. Stories are like these randomly displayed dots. They are useful and meaningful, but only if you can allow them to be there as they are without focusing on them. Then by looking through them tenderly suddenly a whole new world opens, a world which will dwarf any story.

Passionate supervision as I see it does not change the outline of a supervision session in obvious ways. The passionate supervisor like in any other form of supervision will talk with the supervisees about their clients. Their stories will be the obvious focus of the work. The dynamics between practitioner and client and the stories will be explored together and other possibilities to intensify and deepen the work will be discussed. This is how traditionally supervision works and this will also happen in passionate supervision.

The new dimension passionate supervision brings into the work comes from the supervisor's presence and passion, not from what actually is talked about in the supervision session.

When I think back of my first experience with the psychotherapist – as mentioned at the beginning of the chapter – it was not what he said or did, but his obvious awareness of and presence in a different space that affected me so deeply.

The passionate supervisor has not merely an intellectual concept of a reality beyond the box, but actually experiences life beyond stories. Similar to a parent he not only knows that life is bigger than what it seems to be, but actually lives in that bigger space. The stories then are merely used similarly to how the randomly placed 2-dimensional dots are used to get to the

3-dimensional picture: they are the starting points to a deeper experience.

In supervision, the stories like the dots are all there are to focus on. They are appreciated. However, by also keeping a loving and determined detachment from the stories the passionate supervisor will create an atmosphere in which the supervisees can slowly disentangle themselves from the involvement in their clients' reality. The passionate supervisor knows that the solution of a given problem cannot be found on the level the problem is presented, and therefore he will not invest much energy in the presented stories. What does this mean?

Imagine you have six matches of equal length and are asked to create four triangles of equal sizes. The solution of this problem cannot be found on the 2-dimensional level. Whatever you do on a flat piece of paper does not lead to the solution. Once you incorporate a 3rd dimension it becomes easy: three matches you leave in a triangle flat on the piece of paper, on top of it you erect a pyramid with the other three matches.

What it means to find a larger context I learnt some years ago when my very close friend became terminally ill. During his last months everybody experienced an immense peace and love radiating from him. He increasingly was less concerned about his illness and future, but became more open to us. Shortly before his death he took me in his arms and said: 'If I had the choice between a healthy body and the love I am surrounded by, I would without a hint of a doubt choose love.' Although this was incomprehensible for my mind at that moment, I could clearly feel this was his reality. He was outside his box. Love and deep feelings of peace and acceptance were holding him on a different level of consciousness. This touched everybody. It was such a powerful experience that even death dwindled in its presence.

The time with him has affected me deeply. Knowing that there is a power in all of us and a level of consciousness, which can make what we have thought of as important totally lose its potency, is indeed a very liberating experience.

Many spiritual traditions point to the importance to stop thinking, to stop the mind's activity. We can try to fight the mind. Or we can find something bigger to take us over and discover how suddenly that what has bothered us loses its power.

The solution of my friend's 'being terminally ill' did not come from having found a cure, but from having discovered something so much more powerful it even dwarfed death. A cure has not been found for him but healing has taken place. He was living his soul, not experiencing life any more through his stories.

There is no tool, no technique to find that peaceful and open place outside the box and beyond the stories. The mind cannot possibly understand or create this place. The mind is always only interested in creating stories. I am not talking about learning something new. I am talking about re-connecting with a place in ourselves, which has always been there, but has been covered up by a huge amount of stories that we have learnt to accept as 'reality'. The passionate supervisor just carefully points to the possibility that stories are just stories, however powerful they may be. This has to be done gently and lovingly; the process itself, though, can be quite fierce, surely challenging, at times painful – and irreversible. That is why I talk about breaking a box, rather than melting or softening it.

In order to explore this a bit further, let us for a moment turn to Aikido, a Japanese Martial Art, which I have been involved with for many years.

Aikido teaches how to use the power of the attacker to one's own advantage. By absorbing the attack one learns to move one's body in such a way that the power of the attack is turned back towards the attacker. The more powerful the attack the stronger the response then becomes. The strength comes from not resisting so that the attacker loses the sense of somebody actually being there to attack. He falls into an empty space. Aikido talks about 'Zanshin', which means stillness, when it tries to explain what this empty space is about. But it is more than stillness and surely not really empty at all. It is a presence that is soft and open, alert, solid, focused, centred and explosive. It is a presence not disturbed or unbalanced even when physically attacked, or when surrounded by difficult or threatening life issues. Zanshin is there when all the attacks, all the problems, all the stories just pass gently through us.

Aikido cannot be taught theoretically; it is not a mental exercise. Through observation, constant repetition and close contact with the teacher, old acquired patterns slowly dissolve to give way to new and more effective behaviour. Aikido is more than a physical exercise. It shows who we are when we welcome life. If we complain about or fight against what is, if we argue with reality, we always lose. By not resisting, but using whatever life throws at us und turning it into our advantage, we radiate a loving, passionate, fierce and fearless energy – an energy which makes passionate supervision possible.

Here are some thoughts about the process of passionate supervision with an organization I have been working with for some years. This organization consists of eight social workers, and is working with the homeless, especially those who are severely destitute and traumatized.

There are no quick fixes when we deal with deep transformation and change. Passionate supervision is always a long-term process. (See Chapter 5, where Joan Wilmot writes about long-term work.) Obviously passionate supervision needs to take into account the day-to-day problems practitioners are experiencing in their work and has to deal with them, but at the same time it is also holding a space for a wider transformation.

In my experience, we all go through a process in our lives, which is quite similar to that of dying. I find it at times helpful for containing and understanding long-term therapeutic work to describe this process in five stages: denial, despair/depression, bargaining, anger and acceptance. That process of course does not go smoothly from one step to the other. Often there is a mixture of any of those stages present. Some groups start off with 'denial': 'Why do we need supervision? We are OK'! This particular group I am going to talk about here clearly started off from 'despair/depression' when I first met them.

This group of social workers was particularly bombarded by constant and ever-increasing demands from their clients. The stories the social workers had to listen and respond to were heart wrenching and often difficult to digest, leaving the group in a kind of chronic state of shock. This resulted in many sick leaves, tension in the team, times of depression, hopelessness and helplessness. There was always a drama to respond to, never really time to sit and be with each other as a team. Similar to the clients they were working with, for them life was just surviving, not living, enjoying and creating.

The first breakthrough in our work together I remember was when one of the social workers spontaneously, with tears welling up in her eyes and softly looking at the group said: 'Hi, you'. It was a moment of waking up and from then on the group began to see and acknowledge each other as individuals – and to work together as a team. Suddenly there was an awareness of space and time for each other. Not just tasks and problems to look at and solve, but a time to be. Over many months other stages of the five-step process came up. For instance 'anger' erupted, then 'denial', questioning what we were actually doing here together. Then 'bargaining' happened, when team members tried to find individual solutions to deal with stress. For instance some withdrew, decided to be less involved, hoping by that to lessen the effect the work has on them. But what we always came back to was this 'Hi, you': recognizing each other, supporting each other, seeing each other. The team became more alive, present and passionate. Passion without stillness and openness leads to fanaticism and ultimately to despair. We discovered how to be still and open even when a war was raging around us. Then the team had to deal with two suicides and one attempted suicide within a week. It was very moving to see them just tenderly holding everybody's feelings and experiences without judging, regretting, criticizing or splitting off. More and more often the team was in the stage of 'acceptance': accepting one's limitations and embracing lovingly the fact that life is so much bigger than we are, that we can never control it, can never really understand it, but we can learn to trust it and gently follow its process. Acceptance is very different to resignation. Resignation is passive. Acceptance is active, alive, taking what comes and embracing it with love and passion, and thereby going beyond the surface story to a deeper level. One team member suggested that she does not see herself any more as a social worker dealing with cases and stories. 'I am a Soulworker, dealing with Souls.' Increasingly the social workers saw less the stories and the pain clients brought to them. They began to see less victims and sufferers, but Souls with their particular and often mysterious journeys.

I am thinking of an experience at Notting Hill Carnival some years ago, where spontaneously I felt this 'acceptance' as mentioned above. It was very crowded and when I left a particular dense spot I discovered my purse had been stolen. Surprisingly the moment of realization was also a moment of total openness and utter peace. There was only a hint of thought, a detached observation: 'Oh, somebody else has got my purse now'. It was an immensely beautiful moment. I felt totally present and totally still. I instantly knew that this is who I really am, the core of myself not covered up by thoughts or feelings.

I could not hold on to it for long, though – but long enough to recognize it. Suddenly, like a dam which had been holding the water back suddenly bursts, all the usual thoughts came flooding in: 'I have been "robbed", somebody has "stolen" all my money, how stupid of me...!' It became obvious to me that it is not life which creates pain. What create pain are our thoughts about it.

Once at home I recalled the experience of openness and no-thought, and the story of 'being robbed' became at least a positive story, in which I had re-discovered something beautiful.

However, although I turned a bad story into a good one about empowerment, ultimately it does not really matter what kind of story I identify with. Story is story, whether good or bad; they are always created in my mind and never show who I really am. Recalling my experience did not bring back what so deeply had touched me. Recalling the story made me feel good and took away my feeling victimized, but it became just another story of something I had experienced and have lost now (the beautiful moment of total acceptance and openness). My box was still intact, although it may have felt a bit more comfortable – and surely more entertaining.

Breaking the box means more than replacing old well-known stories with new and exciting ones. It is a challenge, especially when one has good, exciting and expanding feelings and experiences to contain, and one must hold them too and not take them so seriously. It does surely not mean we cannot be really sad or really happy any more. Maybe the opposite is true. However, we become more able to observe tenderly our feelings and thoughts without allowing them to take us over.

Passionate supervision does not help to make boxes more comfortable. It is not interested in helping to survive the one battle. Passionate supervision supports the process of breaking boxes for good.

We do experience many moments when we are outside our box. However, we usually do not give attention to these split seconds, and do not have the presence and awareness for catching them, since we are so focused on and occupied with our thoughts and feelings, and so seduced by our stories.

There is an experiment in which you are shown a short video of two groups of people on either side of the screen throwing balls to each other. Your task is to count the balls. At the end of the video you are asked whether you have seen something unusual. It is highly unlikely you have. But actually a huge gorilla has walked twice from one side of the screen to the other, stopping in the middle and hammering his chest with his fists. You did not see the gorilla because you were too busy counting.

In passionate supervision an atmosphere is created, in which supervisor and supervisee together can deepen their presence and can look and watch without being distracted by preconceived ideas, expectations and stories. 'Looking' and 'not knowing' are intrinsically human qualities. I believe that they are in fact our essence, and exert an enormous power for expansion, transformation and liberation when done in a spirit of alertness, openness, love and passion.

In the following I will write about my experience of working for the Medical Foundation in London in a project called 'Natural Growth Project' (NGP), with refugees and asylum seekers who have survived torture. It does not describe my work as a supervisor as such. Nevertheless it is a good example of what can happen when we create a space, in which we are not distracted by thoughts and stories. These clients have changed my outlook on what I believe psychotherapy can be about, and have challenged me to look for Soul rather than for stories. This has helped me deepen my own awareness and understanding of passionate supervision.

These clients have come to this country severely traumatized. Most of them hardly speak English. They are living in an intense painful box, in a terrible nightmare. The stories they tell are truly horrific. These stories and the pain they are experiencing need of course to be acknowledged and talked about (we are supported by interpreters at times) and a lot of practical help is required. However, if we only saw the wounding, we merely would strengthen the part in them that feels victimized, pained and in need of support. These clients are far more than their wounds. I believe there is a place in all of us that is far deeper than all our stories, all our thoughts and all our wounds; we are far more than our worst nightmares and fears. This place I have called 'Soul'.

The work of the NGP is about giving space to Soul; it is not about healing wounds. The NGP has two projects run by a group analyst, a gardener/project worker, administrator and myself as a psychotherapist on a part-time basis. They are the Garden Project, which is adjunct to the Medical Foundation in London and the Allotment Project, which I am going to refer to here. In the Allotment Project we have rented about 16 plots of land in two different allotment sites in London. We work with more than 25 individuals, couples and families. Each individual or family can be on the allotment and cultivate whenever and whatever they want. Once a week I, together with the gardener, would meet these clients for a day on the allotment.

Nature is a wonderful aid. Digging the soil, planting the seeds, doing what needs to be done on the allotment and waiting for things to happen can become so deeply engaging and so wonderfully containing and holding, that it distracts us from our thoughts and stories – even if it is only for a while. When we apply the idea of passionate supervision as discussed above, the psychotherapist's task is to stay open, alert and present. He makes sure not to get seduced by stories and not to get pushed into believing that he is dealing with anything else but powerful Souls. Nothing else really needs to happen.

Souls are like seeds. A seed needs tender care, good soil, some water and light and lots of warmth. It does not need pulling or pushing, or wise words to encourage it to break through the surface. It does not even need constant attention. For its growth it actually does not need the gardener. When the time is right it will show itself. When the time is right, Soul will stir and break through the box.

Here a short report:

The psychiatrist described 'B' as 'severely paranoid depressive', with an inability to make or sustain contact, muteness and a total dependency on support from his family. He is experiencing frequent panic attacks, especially when in closed spaces like buses or even at home, when windows cannot be opened wide enough. He mostly stays in bed at home, and leaves the house only to come to the allotment.

'B' comes for many weeks and just sits on his plot without doing anything. He just sits and I sometimes sit with him. Nothing seems to happen. I am just with him, holding 'his box' without interfering with it, being with him without expectations and working with him without intentions. Then one day he discovers a ladybird. This is the first moment something is acknowledged outside his own body and the first thing he relates to. Some weeks later I observe him chasing birds off his plot. He is protecting his space, which has become slightly bigger again.

And then many months later a moment I will never forget. It is a very hot day. 'B' is watering his garden with a hose. I playfully encourage him to splash my feet. He does it in his usual way: stone-faced, eyes frozen in fear. And suddenly it happens. A spark appears in his eyes – and Soul is shining through. As if somebody has switched the light on. He then turns the hose at me and completely soaks me head to toe, roaring with laughter. I am totally stunned, not comprehending what is happening and deeply moved at the same time. Those who witness it are in tears. What then follows is nearly as touching: 'B' sits with me for more than an hour and talks and talks and talks. I do not understand a word, because he speaks in his language – but it does not matter at all. It feels better like that, since it prevents me from thinking and analysing. It makes it easier to be with him and enjoy the flow of energy, which was stuck inside him for so many years.

Soul can never be reached with our mind; it is far bigger than any story, but always there, like a seed, hidden, yet full of energy, waiting to break through when the time is right. It has an amazing strength. As a seed can open even the hardest surface, Soul can create love even in the darkest places. When Soul shines it seems to touch and awake the Soul in everybody around. It reaches places far deeper than any story. It silences any thoughts. It breaks any box. When Soul shines we seem to contact a realm which is utterly peaceful, a realm where we are connected with each other, with nature and life in a most beautiful and liberating way.

Intense experiences in life, especially traumatic and painful ones, can take over our entire life, colouring every façade of it, hold and imprison us every single day.

They can be like dreams we cannot shake off, or like nightmares persecuting and rattling us night after night. But they only stay powerful as long as we are asleep. The moment we wake up dreams lose their impact. We may still feel breathless after a nightmare, may even want to talk about it with somebody, but we can slowly recover from it, because it only has been a bad dream. We can stop identifying with it and confusing it with 'reality'.

Dreams appear totally realistic as long as we stay in them. When we wake up we leave our dreams behind. The same is true for our stories and worries. As long as we stay in our box they appear to be real. When we wake up to Soul, we then can leave them behind and recognize them for what they really are. Then true healing can happen. True healing is the recognition that the wounding we have experienced actually never has occurred. True healing can only happen when we touch Soul. Without the experience of Soul, healing becomes merely an attempt to comfort the dreamer, rather than to wake him up.

Dreams always end. At one point we always leave them behind once we have woken up from them. The same is true for our stories. Sooner or later we leave them behind as well – at the latest when death finally breaks the box and our last story ends.

Is not life's greatest secret to break the box earlier, to wake up to Soul as our true self – and find that death does not exist?

I believe we are living in a time in which it is no longer the privilege of the very few to break their boxes and to set themselves free. All of us can do it now in our individual and unique ways. We do not need to belong to a certain religion, identify with a specific belief system, we do not need to have meditated in remote caves for many years. We only have to look at our own stories – and see them for what they are.

With that passionate supervision becomes something more than what we offer to others or what is being done to us. It becomes an urgent task and an immensely exciting adventure.

Introduction to Chapter 2

Julie's work gives us a broad sweep of the range of supervision, from her experience as a long-standing supervisor and founder of a training institute in supervision, and from someone who greatly benefited from supervision in her early years herself. She mentions the soul and heart, the context and the ecology of supervision, and how these enter into the supervisory encounter. Her passion for the range of opportunities that supervision offers, particularly the potential for learning, are at the heart of this piece.

When I asked Julie what she most wanted to share from writing this chapter she said:

A love of learning,
A permission to take the whole of our experience into the supervisory space.
To continue to learn from each other.
To know that in supervision there can be the secondary gain of an educationally needed repair.
To continue to be curious, about everything!
To keep being green and juicy.

Chapter 2

Passionate Supervision:
A Wider Landscape
Julie Hewson

In this chapter I seek to engage the reader in the delight and challenge of taking into account the fuller educative function of a rich supervisory relationship. I offer an opportunity to consider the culture, history, literature, context and ecology of supervision; and also a chance to create, what I call an educational repair as well as stretch the horizons of those seeking the highest quality service in the field.

On a windy and grey November day, I sit and find myself writing passionately about supervision, the strange juxtaposition of the cold external world and the sense of supervision as being an oasis or a fireside, a place where a weary traveller can take some respite and nourishment to continue his or her professional journey.

My experience of the very best of supervision was an educationally needed developmental repair. I had missed out on a large chunk of concrete operational thinking when I was at primary school, with the result that I couldn't always explain how I had got from A to B. My intuition was good, my rationale and the outcome were often accurate, but the bridge was missing.

My supervisor helped me name and categorize in a way that was new to me. It stopped me feeling ashamed.

Shame is a belief that there is something wrong with us; for example it may be an existential decision based on early toxic experiences, it may be based on educational gaps in learning processes, it may be based on the fact that the person being supervised is more knowledgeable than the supervisor, it could be a combination of various factors. Whatever it is, it can, as my research has shown, get in the way of a healthy relational supervisory/mentoring process. It does indicate how important the nature of the relationship is in any adult learning situation (Unpublished thesis Hewson 2001).

The supervisory relationship is one that can be educative, supportive, growthful, challenging and collegial. It is educative in that it provides a forum for research and to read more widely; supportive in that it provides a hand or an ear during the discovery process; growthful in that at its best it should increase our resources; challenging because it takes us out of our comfort zone; and collegial as it is a relationship of equals, albeit one more resourced than the other. I see it as a mutual learning, a relationship of great potential creativity. At its very best it redresses that which is lacking in ordinary training experiences, even extraordinary ones. It gives us a chance to explore our understanding of concepts and their application, of the effect our clients have on us, of existential issues and at times our own despair.

At the time of writing this I had just returned from examining a number of extraordinary people whose life experiences had shaped them in a way that was outside my realm of experience. This was in Prague at the Czech Institute of Supervision. It was a rich and humbling experience because even though I was the assessor, I learned as much from them as they did from me. One woman we examined had come through her suffering during the Communist era, having been forced to turn her back on her chosen profession and had gone into a completely different field, because of the political status of her family. It meant that she was not allowed to go to university, so she became an engineer instead. In her fifties, after the revolution ousted the Soviets, she trained as a psychologist and then a supervisor of clinical psychologists. She is currently supervising the work of those engaged in helping refugees. It was moving to hear her describe how she felt an understanding of displaced persons from her own experiences under Communist rule, and also from her knowledge of her own family history which showed that most had been decimated at Auschwitz.

In her viva voce she demonstrated that supervision did not take place in a bubble. She delivered the narrative of supervision in her exam; the history, the politics, the spirituality, the existential nature and the humility of supervision. She did this by the joy in her work, in her compassion and courage. She spoke matter of factly about the work of her supervisees with often quite harrowing stories. She didn't over-dramatize; instead she spoke of respect and a real felt sense of the situations she was supervising. (There are similarities here with the work described by Jochen Encke in the previous chapter.) It reminded me of a Dutch Jewish psychiatrist who used to work with victims of torture. When I remarked that he seemed to carry these horrors with a lightness of being without in any way minimizing the reality of the suffering, he said, 'Ah well I think, as a boy, I was inoculated against some of it in the Second World War'.

As with this man, I found that I was deeply moved by the Czech psychologist's supervisory work and sense of being. What it showed us was the significance of her history, how through it she modelled endurance, courage and steadfastness, and in spite of all, a gentle optimism about the possibilities of success and change. These are great qualities in a supervisor, and this woman in addition had a quiet humility and great sense of humour, again sterling qualities in such a critical role. It was as if by her very presence she was showing her supervisees that all things are possible, and that human beings endure against all odds.

Passionate supervision is about the humanity of the practitioner. Clients can engender difficult feelings. Staying open and not shutting down and becoming detached, cynical, or bored requires a lively and safe forum in which to address our countertransference.

Individual supervision can give us a boundaried space to explore the shadow side of our reactions to our clients, to say the unsayable, to recognize the unthinkable, as well as to honour and respect and feel genuine compassion for the suffering and pain of the people we see. It also gives us a glimpse of our shadow, our overemphasis on intuition and other professional pitfalls, for example our tendency to manage people's lives, our inclination to want the best for people, or looking out of the same window rather too often.

Ten years ago I supervised someone who had been working with a lesbian couple, where there had been serious difficulties in relation to the two young children that one of the couple already had. The partner without children of her own showed jealousy, competitiveness and had even expressed that she wished that they did not exist at all. The couple, who had been together for five years, had tried to communicate about this with each other, without success. My supervisee found that she was becoming increasingly sympathetic to the mother of the children.

On the second session, there was talk of their having a child together through artificial insemination, where both women would have a parenting role from the outset. However, the degree of hostility to the existing children and the levels of emotional violence had led my supervisee to suggest that the couple take time out, and that the mother return to her family home to consider her options.

The supervisee believed that having another child in these circumstances would not be conducive to the well-being of either of the other two children or the new baby. She had unwittingly fallen into the trap of managing other people's lives. As she reported her feelings it became clear that she had taken on her client's emotional state and had become frightened. She believed she had been even-handed and fair in her dealings with both women and had done everything by the book in terms of contracting; nevertheless at the psychological level the female client without children felt she had been discriminated against, and subsequently went on to make a complaint.

Taking supervision for my supervision, I realized that my supervisee was unconscious of the discrimination she had exercised against the emotionally competitive member of the relationship. What she had failed to notice was how she had been manipulated by the mother, who wanted a reason to end the relationship, and the therapist's unwitting collusion had made that possible. At the same time, there was the reality of emotional abuse which had led my supervisee to justify to herself that her actions were appropriate.

Through supervision, I realized I had been stuck in a parallel process of protection, as I wanted to defend my supervisee in the upcoming complaint. This showed me how important my own supervision still is. Understanding the parallel process diffused the situation greatly and I was able to challenge her gently as to the shadow that she was not acknowledging. Although this was not easy for her, she was honest enough to reflect on the grain of truth in the complaint, and this enabled her to become less internally defensive. This put her back in touch with the compassion she had genuinely felt for both parties, although she had seen one as more culpable than the other: it was as if there was the invitation for collusion to go up the chain and the appropriate challenge was needed to come down. It would have been much harder if we had not had such a good relationship, and I shall return to this later. (It also occurs as a theme in many of the chapters in this book.)

Our earliest experiences provide an imprint, and are used as role models for later development. That is why at the beginning of supervision it is important to have a person who is passionate about their work. To have someone supervise you who loves her work and is deeply curious and interested in yours is a stimulating and joyful place to start. Because of my earlier experiences, of gaps in my primary school education, which were brilliantly later compensated for in my grammar school days, I am a passionate believer in how education can be life-enhancing professionally and personally and good supervision can offer that service. Unfortunately these days, educational opportunities are often sacrificed at the altar of short-term expediency, in schools, universities and trainings. With the national curriculum and prescribed competencies, the wonder of a renaissance education has all but disappeared. I am of the generation where such an education was still possible, and I take with me into the supervisory and coaching relationship a passion for the breadth and depth of education, not merely a training.

For the rest of the chapter I will be looking at passionate supervision under the following headings: the soul of supervision, the heart of supervision, the context including the politics, and sociology of supervision and the ecology of supervision. Many of these headings have arisen from passionate discussions with my supervision students. We have argued about the ecology of our profession, as well as the politics of power-based relationships, dual managerial/clinical roles and cultural differences.

Working in different countries and with different generations has helped me to recognize all of the above. This also includes my own aging process. It is easy to forget that the zeitgeist of our era is dramatically different from that of the people we are supervising. I am of the generation of 'baby boomers', post-war infants, who were teenagers in the 1960s, and lived at a time when everything was possible. This was a different world from those born in the 1960s, 1970s and 1980s. The accident of birth determines our perception of the world and our place in it. I remember reading the novel *The Bookseller from Kabul* (Seierstad 2003); I had a client who lived between two worlds, one Afghani and the other westernized. He was endeavouring to make a choice between marrying an educated Afghani professional woman, or continuing to live his life as a free-wheeling western playboy. Reading that book gave me some insight into some of the restrictions both he and his potential bride faced in getting to know each other before the knots were tied. This is one of many ways in which literature has informed my practice.

While working in Eastern Europe the novels of Milan Kundera helped me understand more of the feeling of life under Communist rule and the bleak existential choices faced by those living under oppression.

I remember once, Maria Gilbert, my former supervisor, talking about humanism being the soft under-belly of existentialism. Kundera's books give one the feel of the starkness of choice. What is also interesting was that I met on a train, a person doing research into the different tonality of the books Kundera wrote in French, in English and in Czech. She had discovered that this gifted linguist wrote entirely differently depending on whether the initial manuscript was in English, Czech or French. This in itself displays a subtlety of perception and felt sense, based on language itself. How much as supervisors do we realize this?

Thus, although most supervisory models are meta-perspectives, we do see things from such a different perspective depending on our social, cultural, political and economic experiences. Supervision is more than a dyadic relationship. It does not take place in a vacuum.

I have talked about the subtlety of language, and the influence of cultural and historical perspectives; I am now going to reflect on the nature of the relationship, something I also feel passionate about.

Earlier I mentioned the importance of an equal relationship, even though one person may be more experienced than the other. It is like walking alongside a colleague sharing stories and insights. People do not just bring their professional psychological perceptions; they may bring their love of gardening, the theatre, books, music and travel to the discussion. I have had delightful times working with drama therapists in supervision, who enact their clients. I have experienced bodyworkers bringing their own bodies to supervision because of the effect their clients have had on them. I have used sand tray as a method of contacting the unconscious processes in the supervisee, and each person brings their own metaphors and similes.

A passionate supervisor will really listen to the language and life experience of the person in front of them, and adapt their own style and language accordingly. This is the mark of true humility.

I would now like to look at what I call *the soul of supervision*. This is what I think as the realm of global awareness, of care and concern for ethical living. It may mean that we need to be potent and speak our truth and listen to the truth of others, to be responsive without compromising our integrity, to be vulnerable without losing sight of our ability to effect change, to be a witness and not a bystander. This is not always easy, as sometimes we may have to take a stand and risk being persecuted for it, as in the example mentioned earlier. The soul of supervision is to respect difference and look for shared understanding; to acknowledge weakness and power and not to exploit either; to wish for the very best for the supervisee, their client, the organization and society at large. Sometimes the only way to do this is to hold all in our hearts and still take a stand. When we supervise from this perspective, we want to learn from those who seek our help as well as share our accumulated wisdom, knowledge and skills. There is a saying in Celtic mythology, the body lives in the soul, not the soul lives in the body. We meet and touch each other at that level more often than we comprehend.

In talking about *the heart of supervision*, I mean the generosity of heart, sharing, resourcing, empathy and accord. It is a place where we acknowledge the human-ness of making mistakes and learning from them, being openhearted and forgiving, both of ourselves and others. People often talk of losing heart, or the heart going out of an organization or setting. This is sometimes a reality, not a metaphor. When generous souls leave an organization or group, one has to ask why. If dedicated professionals with a vocation lose heart and begin to suffer burnout, again we need to ask why. I have found that I lose heart when I have done the best I could and still have not achieved all I hoped I would. This is most likely to occur when I have been misunderstood and unappreciated.

Supervision from the heart is about healing, about feeling, and is about enabling the work of the heart to continue. If we look at the NHS and how many dedicated professionals are suffering, or social services, education and those organizations that purport to serve humanity, we see how the heart has been taken out of the profession by fear (see Chapter 10 on Fear and Love). So many of them have been knocked off-centre, by changes in policies, changes in the law, the effects of the shadow side of our societies and litigation. These are things about which we rarely speak in a healthy forum, but which are often addressed in the context of a media circus with particular agendas, or a political or religious bias.

How can we supervise from a good heart? First we need to take care of our heart. In discussion with a good friend of mine who is a psychiatrist, I chided him gently about how he gave all his goodness of heart away to his patients, so there was not much left for himself. In practical terms this led to the over-looking of some important issues which though small in themselves came back to create some quite serious chaos in his personal life. The over-used phrase work–life balance does have meaning here. We truly do need to take care of our hearts and nourish ourselves through those activities each of us knows are good for us. We need to model to our supervisees that there is a life outside work.

In considering *the context of supervision*, I am thinking about organizations, professions and three or multi-handed con-tracts, as well as the sociology, economics and politics of the same. Recently, for example, there was a commission for one of my supervisees to provide some in-depth training for a group of professionals. What he didn't know was that there had been a year of negotiation within the agency, prior to his invitation, and that what the participants had wanted was different from what he had been asked to provide. This is an example of a multi-handed contract going off-track, with subsequent conse-quences for all concerned. I have written about this elsewhere (Hewson 2001).

In essence, the ethos of certain professions, organizations and groups need to be taken seriously. One size does not fit all and an awareness of the value base and culture of the organization within which you might be supervising is absolutely essential. I suggest the supervisor may have to don the guise of an anthropologist and tread carefully until they understand the subtleties of the culture they are entering. For example I suggest that the supervisors I train imagine they were from another planet. Eric Berne, the founder of Transactional Analysis, encouraged people to think Martian. Context includes the ecology, the sociology, the economics and politics of supervision. For example, sometimes people speak as though supervision was a luxury, a soft option that could be dispensed with in times of financial constraint. We can't afford it is the frequently heard cry; you can't afford not to is all too often the reality. The economics and the sociology of supervision refer to a culture where such skills are sometimes referred to as soft skills, when in fact they are central to the success of any organization which employs people!

Politics has a range of meanings, all associated with the underlying concept of power. There is always the perennial one of the dual roles that some people have to perform of clinical or case supervisor and line management. This has proved to cause no end of difficulties for both supervisor and supervisee alike. In parts of Devon the two roles were separated in social services, to the great relief of all concerned. In the NHS it is certainly not often the case, and it has been known to lead to practitioners not divulging that they do not fully understand a procedure in case they are seen as incompetent. In a sad case several years ago, in an intensive care baby unit, such a situation had tragic consequences.

The ecology of supervision requires an awareness of the greater picture, our planet, our societies, our care or lack of it one for another. In these times when the technology allows us to witness events world wide, we can no longer ignore the effects of our actions in the wider context. Here we need to consider passionately where we are focusing our energies, to what end, for whose benefit. We need to look up sometimes and see the wider picture and ask ourselves are there any ecological factors we have not taken into account in our work in supervising. If for example, we are supervising or coaching a senior executive in a company whose stated aims are to make money no matter what the cost to the environment, or to the well-being of underpaid and exploited individuals in the third world, we as professionals need to consider the ecology of our professional role. This may require us to attend closely to our core values, to believe we can operate from a place of total integrity and perhaps make a difference. The areas of ecology politics and spirituality overlap.

I remember vividly the *sociological* manifestation of the effects of societal norms associated with education during the Soviet take-over of what was then Czechoslovakia. I can see to this day a colleague who was preparing for her professional exam, standing up like a nine-year-old, answering questions, over-detailing and behaving in a way that would ensure her failure in the world of the autonomous west. She would have been seen as over-adapting and operating from a regressed child-like position, which would not have inspired confidence in her professional capability. What we would call over-detailing was once considered a virtue in Czech schooling. In the profession to which she was endeavouring to belong it looked like an attempt to be understood from a child-like position, not from one where certain parameters were understood, from an adult perspective.

I have found that not only travel, but reading foreign literature, going to art house films, looking at cartoons and even advertisements from different cultures have all helped me in gaining some insight and understanding about difference. They have given me a wonderful opportunity to widen my horizon in the name of continuing professional development. They have helped me look at things from many perspectives, to not make assumptions, to want to understand another way of looking at the world, listening to it, getting a sense of it.

In conclusion, at the heart of passionate supervision is the multi-faceted nature of the relationship. We might start as mentor, then coach, then supervisor; we might need to champion our supervisee as well as resource and educate him or her. We might need to be silent and just listen, to allow the space for free flow of ideas, emotions, thoughts and experiences. We might need to walk behind sometimes and at others alongside. Occasionally we might need to step in front to ward off danger, as described in the earlier case example.

What is clear to me, as I consider what it is that makes me so passionate about supervision, is that not only are we caring for our supervisees, clients, patients and customers, but we are also engaged in the teaching and development process of the individual professional. We cannot do that without considering the context, the politics, the ecology and the heart and soul of the work.

Let us just for a moment consider what kind of metaphor we could use for this professional relationship. We might ask ourselves what particular kind of animal is this thing called supervision. In its way it can range across prairies, climb mountains, swim into the depths and fly close to the sun. We need to be courageous as well as ethical if we are going to practise passionate supervision. Part of our challenge is to continue our own exploration and challenge our own comfort zones as supervisors, as well as staying steady and true. Part of this process is a willingness to learn from those we supervise. Supervision can be a joy or a total nightmare. I recently discovered that the Institute that I founded has moved to a beautiful building in which many years ago, they used to carve both angels and gargoyles for the cathedral. I suppose that is our challenge, to recognize both, befriend both and contain both. What a challenge!

Reference

Seierstad, A. (2003) *The Bookseller of Kabul*. London: Little Brown and Company.

Further reading

Carroll, M. and Tholstrup, M. (2001) *Integrative Approaches to Supervision*. London: Jessica Kingsley Publishers.

Hewson, J.A. (2001) *Shame in Supervision*. Unpublished paper, research based.

Carroll, M. and Holloway, E. (1999) *Counselling Supervision in Context*. London: Sage.

Carroll, M. and Holloway, E. (1999) *Training Counselling Supervisors*. London: Sage.

Whitehead, E.E. and Whitehead, J.D. (2003) *Shadows of the Heart: A Spirituality of the Painful Emotions*. Lincoln, NE: iUniverse.

Introduction to Chapter 3

For David, passionate supervision is a way of ensuring that we can continue to grow and take risks, and not allow ourselves to become part of a system that would, in his words, dull our sensitivity and limit our responses. Physician, heal thyself is the core of the chapter, and he describes how in supervision he had to, as a doctor, face his omnipotent wish to heal.

When I asked David what he most wanted the reader to get from reading his chapter he replied:

> An insight into how supervision has changed the way I work and a sense that you (the reader) are not alone. He believes that realizing others have grown by reflecting on their uncertainty will encourage you to take more risks in your supervision and be more confident that your greatest challenges can be reframed as your biggest opportunities.

Chapter 3

The 'Ah Ha' Moment
Passionate Supervision as a Tool for Transformation and Metamorphosis
David Owen

This chapter is about the transformative value of passionate supervision and is informed by insight from my own personal and professional development, based on the experiences I have had as a medical doctor, homeopathic physician, educator, supervisee and supervisor. Passionate supervision puts development, growth and transformation at the heart of the supervision relationship. It is not a tool for control but a means of inquiry.

In this chapter I will share and explore the transformative nature of passionate supervision. You will see why I believe passionate supervision is the place to take risks, to go beyond our comfort zones and to prevent ourselves becoming part of a system that dulls our sensitivity and limits our responses. It is a tool that serves both our personal and professional growth and reveals the intimate connection between our inner nature and our outer work.

Introduction

Change and challenge are an inevitable part of being in practice. We can only choose to embrace it or resist it. It is all too easy for us as supervisors and supervisees to focus our work together on trying to maintain the status quo. There are times when we need support and times when we need to learn from those with more experience, but if we are not careful, resisting change forces what is struggling to emerge to stay hidden. By responding courageously to our clinical challenges and welcoming the opportunity for transformation, we grow and develop in our awareness of our self and our ability to function usefully and with insight into our life's work.

Passionate supervision offers both supervisee and supervisor opportunities to develop new understandings about themselves. They move towards deeper and clearer insights into their world. Passionate 'super-vision' is more than reflecting about yourself. It is where you can see, meet and get to know new aspects of yourself. It is not just a matter of gaining an elevated perspective like standing on a stepladder, but more like seeing the world in new ways as if through new eyes. (Sheila Ryan goes into this in more detail in Chapter 4.)

Having experienced many styles of supervision, I know the importance of weaving together the appropriate knowledge, the best support in learning new skills and the personal development necessary to sustain each of us in the fire of our work as a healthcare professional. When this balance is wrong, as I believe it is for many healthcare professionals at the moment, then the work we do with the health of others gives rise to overwhelming challenges and unsustainable stresses to ourselves, including jeopardizing our own health. It corrupts responsibility and stunts the development of our professions, making it difficult for us to change or exercise our 'ability to respond' freely to the opportunities and the privilege our work with others offers. Here is a personal story that illustrates a transformation I experienced in supervision that significantly reframed how I approach my work and relate to patients.

Treating the last patient

As well as recovery, joy and birth, our work as practitioners brings experiences of suffering, pain and death. If these are not integrated into our psyche they move the healer to the edge of society. For 20 years I was educated to use tools first to heal patients and then to help patients heal themselves. I had the benefit of much educational input including mentoring, tutoring and supervision. I, like many other carers, had episodes of being exhausted and drained by my work; at times I felt alone in my profession and isolated from my community. I identified and built a network of support from colleagues, friends and family, including supervisory groups where it was possible to share what I was finding hard, and the realization that I was not alone gave me the confidence to explore how I felt and why.

By starting to engage in what I would now call transformative or passionate supervision I began to see that the things I found most difficult potentially had most to offer me, that my difficult cases provided the biggest opportunity to my own development, some might say for my own healing. It was receiving supervision on one particular lady whose need for maintenance, not cure, overwhelmed me with feelings of inadequacy that led to me realizing that not everyone needs a cure. I realized that part of me had secretly believed that if I did my job properly 'I would one day cure the last patient...' and at one level I had bought into the thought that 'one day the waiting room would be empty if I did my job right'. No wonder I was stressed. I felt that each patient not cured demonstrated a failure, each difficulty was an obstruction to my professional calling and competence, and that all suffering was something I was partly responsible for. Realizing instead that illness would always exist and that it served a deep and important function to individuals, society and our culture was fundamental to my personal development and this was an 'ah ha' moment in reframing my core beliefs. Obviously I had been educated about the incidence and prevalence of illness; I had been supported in using my profession's tools to work, but at a deeper level I had built my practice on the belief (or illusion) that one day my job would be done, that the task could be completed.

Indeed it was important to me to realize that those cases I found most difficult were not those where I needed more knowledge or skills, or those where I needed some additional support. These are important and have their place, but rather the most difficult cases are paradoxically those that require the deepest personal shift and in turn offer the opportunity for the deepest personal development and professional transformation. If our professions or our personal awareness cannot change, we find health professionals that struggle to manage change and diversity, and healers who become fixated and entrenched in their opinions. This leads to a health service and healers who themselves are sick. The ongoing development and at times regular metamorphosis required by each of us in the healing professions is central, both for the supervisee and supervisor, in passionate supervision. The potential for transformation is at the very heart of the supervisory relationship in passionate supervision. It can be challenging and painful as much growth is, but it is not necessarily something you need to feel alone with. Challenge is as much part of growth as suffering is part of staying healthy.

There are times when I have, despite a caring and compassionate style of supervision, found a supervisee or supervisor just too challenged by a situation to move through it. Often these issues reoccur for the supervisee or supervisor in different settings. It is as if they are on the brink of dealing with something that is quite major for them. For example, in group supervision I remember a participant who had reoccurring issues about relationships with patients. She had had major illness herself (breast cancer) and as a child had a traumatic relationship with her parents, especially her mother, that had never been resolved. In a group setting she seemed unable to explore her need, but rather required unconditional support and 'holding' by the group. Up to a point the group could provide this but after a time the group wanted to move beyond it. The supervisee and supervisor were unable to work in the group on this and instead the group split in that session, and also failed to convene again. I hope the supervisee found somewhere the issue could surface in a way that could be transcended.

I subsequently realized the supervisor had difficulty in dealing with issues in relation to mothers, despite their frequently coming up. I expect this continued until she was able to take this to her own supervision. Although the emotional release and pleasure when insights are made are profound or even ecstatic, I would not want you to think it is always easy. Often there is a period of discomfort, or even pain while these issues struggle to emerge from the unconscious. Recognizing the opportunity and developing the skills and courage to face such issues is why this book has been written.

I have already mentioned the importance of education and support in supervision and this is well catered for, although there are still too many groups of health professionals where even this is not adequately or routinely provided. However, the developmental and transformative role, beyond the mere sequential addition of facts or experience, is key to staying a vibrant, healthy, well-developed practitioner. I suspect it is at times overlooked or avoided because supervisees choose 'not to go there' or supervisors prefer to keep to what they know. However, at other times it can seem that the sort of transformative supervision championed in this book is conspired against by those who have strong political, ideological and financial reasons for resisting change. Transformative supervision and other reflective and enabling tools of change are not just at the heart of personal insight and awareness, but are at the core of how we practice clinically and central to the ethos and values of our professional organizations. Among other things they are a vital part of enabling a health carer to be fully present with a client or patient. And whatever aspect of healthcare you are involved in it enables our regulatory, representative and training organizations to establish what it is to be a professional.

Reflection point

Think of a major insight or 'ah ha' moment you have had. What made this possible and how did it transform your practice?

Reframing what we find difficult

Various styles, models and types of supervision are increasingly being used as tools for training, enhancing performance, maintaining professionalism, for qualification (both as a requirement to qualify and as a form of assessment), to regulate and manage practices and to support individual practitioners. In my experience a lot of supervision models are failing to meet the real and deepest needs of therapists and practitioners. I see passionate supervision as a way of breaking out of what Jochen Encke in Chapter 1 has described as the self-imposed box that we allow to confine us, so that we can begin addressing the otherwise unmet needs that lie behind our fears. These unmet and frequently unconscious needs are often why some individuals hold back in some way from really hearing the unconscious needs of others or from stepping into their power and offering transformative change to others.

Passionate supervision, with its emphasis on transformation as much as the supportive and educative roles of supervision, is one way of refocusing on the growth, change and development that supervision potentially offers both to the individual and to the organizations that we work in or that regulate us. In this book we are looking at supervision, but I suspect this desire to grow through our challenges is behind the growth in mentoring and coaching. In this chapter I have chosen to champion particularly the personal development aspect of passionate supervision and its ability to help with 'difficult issues', but it is just as able to transform your clinical practice, the way we work with colleagues and the way our professional organizations operate. Imagine how it could be if every difficult case revealed more to you than easy ones, if each struggle enabled your practice to grow, if your colleagues celebrated with you the hard things, and your professional organization felt enabled to reframe the challenges they faced as opportunities for growth and change.

In practice, the most dramatic transformation happens when long-held assumptions no longer make sense in light of experience. These are sometimes experienced as an 'oh no' feeling that might be why an issue is taken to supervision. When a realization comes flooding it may be experienced as an 'ah ha' feeling with a corresponding shift in long-held assumption, values and behaviour. A common example in supervision is the first time a supervisee 'clicks' that a person they are finding difficult to understand is projecting certain characteristics on to them, for example the client who transfers on to the therapist, characteristics that belong to the client's parents. Not all examples are so dramatic; some dawn more gradually and a reframing takes place through a series of smaller insights giving an ahhhh…ahhhh type feeling. For example the gradual realization that the supervisee has that an unresolved relationship with a parent colours not only how they see a client but even the sort of clients they 'draw to them'.

Sometimes significant transformative changes take place gradually over years and are only really noticeable on looking back. One might even suggest that when well-integrated into professional training and as part of the ongoing development of a professional, they should be managed in small 'bite size' chunks. For me such an example of gradual insight has happened around the timing and length of consultations. There has not been a single moment when this was completely reframed; rather a collection of insights, some as a supervisee, some as a supervisor, has led to a shift in how I see time issues including running late, keeping patients waiting (and patients arriving late), filling breaks with numerous tasks, etc. I gradually realized that time keeping is one of the ways I can be controlling with patients. This contributed to the realization that defining how much could be achieved in a consultation was limited to the time I had available was only one view. Seeing this with super-vision has gradually led to a different view about length of consultation that has fundamentally contributed to how I structure my practice. This had huge implications on the professional and organizational models I have looked to and explored in delivering care. I had chosen to work with appointments a certain length to define (and even limit) the intimacy, depth and expectations of clients and patients. That I had chosen this by choosing the organizational structure I was working in was as equally valid as seeing it as determined by my job, and that the way it had been done by others was the way I had to do it now. This has helped me to see that the way I want to work is ultimately expressed in how I work; the apparent reasons for having to do it in a particular way are really manifestations of my own unconscious and of choices I make.

In this way our personal lives or practices and our professional organizations each interconnect.

With this in mind, it might be interesting for you to reflect on your experience of transformative change in your supervision practice and how the delivery of your supervision is structured. In this and other reflective exercises in this chapter I invite you to 'try out' different answers. Often our first answer will be only a small step from what we have experienced or know; the second an answer we imagine might be given by someone who is more experienced or knows more. It is the third answer, the one you can dare yourself to think, that at first might seem outlandish, that might be paradoxically opposite or at an extreme from your first answer that might offer you most.

Reflection point

If supervision were to be more transformative than it currently is for you, how would you need to change, how would your supervisor be different and how might your professional organization alter in its view of or the provision of supervision?

The different roles of the supervisory relationship

Supervision has a number of roles sometimes described as educative, supportive and managerial. However, these descriptions fail to reflect the importance of the developmental role of supervision. Educative supervision alone is often about reaching and maintaining a particular perspective, about 'best practice'. Managerial supervision alone is often provided on behalf of organizations and focused on 'quality control'. Supportive supervision alone is often about helping you to return to, to recover or restore a perspective to deliver 'more of the same'. If the focus is to 'recover' sometimes the impetus to 'discover' is lost; supervision can become the 'sticking plaster' for the therapist rather than growing and developing through the healing opportunity that is presented.

Each role of supervision has its place and can be balanced in a way that is helpful for the individual, their practice and their professional organization. However, none adequately describes the important transformative role of supervision. Without this transformative role, supervision can concentrate too much on getting everyone in a profession or organization up to a certain level without tapping the potential of the individual to excel beyond the norm. It can focus so much on restoring the foundations that it can inhibit those who are ready to go beyond these foundations or it can become so obsessed about mistakes it can paralyse those ready to take a chance on being different. While being professional requires certain norms and boundaries it is important not to let yourself grow stilted and be overwhelmed by difficulties. My passion is for supervision that can help us embrace growth and develop professionally.

For myself an important bit of transformative supervision took place when I recognized the parallel process between my personal development, my professional development and my development as a doctor. I realized early on in my practice that I learnt more from patients, clients, students and supervisees that were not straightforward or easy. It was liberating to share with others that it was not all easy and the struggle to understand things was part of not only how I learnt but also my personal growth. It at first surprised me when I realized that discussing a difficult case caused feelings to arise in me that mirrored those in the patient. It didn't take long to realize there were many similarities between my struggling to understand a difficult case and the struggle that patients' symptoms represented. One such realization was that in the same way as my development was ongoing, so health was a dynamic state. Struggling with a question and the answer were not opposites but two sides of the same thing. In the same way I realized that health and illness are not opposites, and that illness is a necessary part of health. This has transformed my view on my role as a doctor and the rather combative way many carers view illness as something to be fought, irradiated or killed off.

Even as I write this I notice I am self-monitoring, on the one hand resisting naming those things I find difficult or feel embarrassed or incompetent about, as if it would reveal too much of myself. On the other hand, I am mindful of making claims of knowledge or insight, in case it somehow portrays me as being ready for the next challenge or even worse, an expert!

Reflection points

Reflect on whether there are any major issues you have experienced and have not taken to supervision. If so what does this tell you about your supervision?

Considering the different roles of supervision described above which are you most comfortable with and which most uncomfortable with? Why do you think this is?

How true for you is the saying 'that the more I know, the more I know I don't know'?

Contracting

Some of the most transformative supervision happens at unexpected times. These changes are hard to contract for by outcome, hence the importance of contracting with deep trust between supervisee and supervisor.

For the supervisor and supervisee, a clear contract between them can help identify the focus of the supervision. It can also protect them. It allows them to explore rationally different techniques and skills while being aware of their limitations and difficulties. The contract can and often does change and be quite different at different sessions. It can also change and be quite dynamic (or fluid) within a session depending on the emphasis at any one moment. If we think of the educative, supportive and developmental roles of supervision mentioned previously, each may have a different emphasis and the contract and other aspects of the supervisory relationship might reflect this. In a more educational contract the relationship often has more of the flavour of teacher and student; in a support role often the flavour is more of a peer one. In a transformative one the flavour of the relationship can be a bit more like student to student...exploring what might happen, trying different attitudes and opinions out, taking a sometimes radically different perspective and letting go of the idea there is one right way. Moving into and contracting for this development work is often unfamiliar to those working predominately with their support and education hats on and so warrants further exploration.

So, for example, when working in a transformative role, the endpoints and outcomes are difficult to predict. It is not like mixing two substances. Rather, it is like a chemical reaction where supervisee and supervisor are both transformed and change their state. The desired outcome may require a quantum leap from the current position that can not be rationally inferred before the process is fully engaged with, so consent itself is process rather than an outcome. Hence, the consent may rather be more conditional about the context (safe and confidential) and relationship (mutual trust) of the supervision. Boundaries may also shift as the individuals and supervisory relationship unfolds. The development of the supervisor and supervisee often goes together and it is as if they are both on a linked but separate journey. If either is failing to develop and grow, then it is important to address this in supervision, to become aware of what is fixed or stuck. In some long-standing supervisory relationships, the deep trust adds to the ability to move through resistance. At other times the 'stuckness' can be a sign that the relationship between supervisor and supervisee needs to shift (see Chapter 5).

I have several times experienced small shifts in boundaries, releasing a great deal of important material, such as an issue has been offered in group supervision just before a break by a supervisee who was trying to avoid the group really looking at the issue. Supervisors often collude with this and can appear reluctant to step over boundaries, frightened to really meet the supervisee or group in the shadow world where the unconscious is glimpsed. It is as if they are unprepared to see themselves as bigger than their boundaries, to break out of their box or to risk going through their fear. When I have experienced the supervisor inviting the supervisee and group to step across this time (or other) boundary I have noticed a profound shift in the supervisory relationship. In one example, a shift in timing allowed a shame issue to be explored more fully. It made conscious the need of the supervisee to feel special and her desire for others in the group to collude with her shame. In a way she was inviting the group to 'feel bad about her' keeping them from their coffee. It allowed the group to address its unspoken resentment in feeling manipulated that the supervisee had been holding for them. And it allowed a significantly deeper trust to emerge and allowed the supervisor to recognize their own and the group's issues about unmet needs and feeling ashamed for having these. Quite a lot learnt for the price of having slightly cold coffee!

> **Reflection point**
>
> What aspects of your supervision do you find it most difficult to contract around? How do you use professional boundaries to protect yourself from having to explore and possibly change these?

Humility to change

Often, to make the deepest changes the relationship between supervisee and supervisor needs to be based on a high level of mutual trust and confidence. There is a need to face and work through things that at first can appear most threatening. For example over several years I had taken issues that I had had with treating 'cancer patients' to supervision. These patients would be seeking support or assistance with their symptoms, often not consciously naming their hope of a cure or their anger with their disease. I had sat with different teachers and supervisors who would suggest different interventions, try this...do that...each had its rationale. I became so keen to do absolutely everything I could that I read the books, I developed a reputation as 'an expert' (always dangerous due to the increased idealization and frequently unconscious power) and started to teach others. I became the advisor of a cancer charity and increasing numbers of patients attended. There never seemed enough time to do everything I wanted in the appointments; they kept running late and when patients deteriorated I got increasingly upset. I felt angry. In 'group supervision' I brought one such case. Being invited to get in touch with what I wanted was truly terrifying for me. To glimpse my own fear of cancer and of no-one being there for me and express this in a way that was witnessed felt at first as if it would invoke the very illness I was so scared of. It was only the quality of the supervisory relationship, knowing that I was loved and that my worst fears and strongest imagined delusions could not diminish me that allowed me to speak. My hope that someone was in control and fear of being judged had led me to unconsciously accept the projections of others who needed me to be in control and to make judgments on their behalf. I had 'bought into' the illusion I could make them better. The omnipotence was seductive; I had lost my perspective and my ability to help, other than by accepting that the patients' projections were diminished. Gaining insight into how to hold authority without arrogance and regaining my humility has allowed me to re-interpret the role I have to offer in these cases and has generally allowed me to see and work with greater insight into patients' fears and anger.

Without these and similar transformative shifts of perspective my clinical work, teaching and supervision would lack passion and wither like a body without a heart. My work would increasingly be dominated by management protocols, training targets or audit tools. However, it is not easy to face those things that both define and confine how we see ourselves and others. To shift from one perspective to another requires a realization about the limitations or drawbacks of the former. In this way with any change there is some grief or loss. I remember a supervisee when they were on the brink of reframing a view that would alter fundamentally how they worked saying, 'If this is true then everything I've done before has been wrong.' I was touched by this frankness and it deepened my connection with the supervisee and at the same time enabled me to re-examine my own fear of change and recognize the courage to not only see but also make changes. As is often the case when a simple but powerful truth is spoken, it allowed us to re-explore our supervision contact; in some ways being able to see a choice already meant the supervisee had shifted their perspective and had freed themselves up to see it was not a question of either/or, rather one about which way, when and for whom. This was what was most important for them at that time. It is worth remembering that this innate conservatism is on the one hand a useful break to change for change's sake, but also a risk to the natural development of an individual, their practice and even their professional body. Guidance through this schism is just one aspect of passionate supervision that is mediated by the relationship between supervisee and supervisor.

Reflection point

What are your three worst fears of passionate supervision and your three best expectations? How do they reflect those aspects of your practice you would most like to examine?

The supervisee–supervisor relationship

That unconscious issues are projected between supervisor and supervisee is well-recognized. When a supervisor begins to apprehend a deeper truth to the supervisee/client story, it is not a passive process, but leads to a deeper contact with reality with unforeseeable consequences. The potential to change and reframe how the supervisor and supervisee see something is a necessary requirement to see a new truth; in this way the pursuit of truth is creative. Absolute truth in complete fullness lies beyond an objective perception. Yet we discern something of it, as soon as we move beyond the passive and particular, towards an active grasp of properties and relations. Whenever a new truth is glimpsed it has unforeseen consequences – new insights, opportunities, discoveries, departures. These shifts are mirrored between the supervisor and supervisee and frequently it is the openness of the supervisor to transformative change that determines the transformative possibilities for the supervisee. The relationship between supervisee and supervisor is nurtured in practice by the supervisor's own supervision and maintained and 'kindled' by the professional organizations that are secure enough to champion passionate supervision. This in turn provides a driving force for discoveries and insights into our practices and the development of our professional organizations.

Reflection Point

To what extent does your pursuit of truth require the development of your insight and self-knowledge? Can transformative supervision and personal development be other than related?

Knowledge, information and wisdom

New information about our work is constantly emerging and can be found in many sources from journals, teachers, colleagues and researchers. In practice we all need to review and where possible integrate this information to constantly develop our knowledge. And our knowledge dynamically interfaces with our skills and attitudes to shape our wisdom. It is all too easy to lose wisdom by focusing on knowledge, and to lose knowledge when overwhelmed by new information. However, it is through 'passionate supervision' that these educational steps can be transformed into quantum changes where insight and wisdom are found and the novice supervisee can metamorphose into the competent practitioner. It is also the place where the supervisor can journey from competent to adept practitioner. Hence it is important for all those who wish to continue their development from competent practitioner to enter the cauldron of passionate supervision as a supervisor while maintaining their own supervision.

Placing knowledge somewhere between wisdom and information puts each in a helpful perspective. Information itself does not confer knowledge, and knowledge itself does not develop wisdom. All information will not be accurate, all knowledge will not be true, but it must serve the truth. Information may be displaced by new information that is more accurate and knowledge can be displaced by new knowledge that is closer to the truth. Knowing the greater truth allows a wise interaction with your reality. At some level we must trust that the issues that we are presented with (and find difficult) are those that offer the greatest transformative opportunities to us at that time. To reframe this, at some level we draw certain difficulties to us at certain times in order to grow through them. We can choose to resist them or accept them as opportunities to change. In the same way as clients and patients frequently bring with them issues that keep reoccurring until a cure at the appropriate level and depth is found, so do supervisees keep recreating situations and draw particular clients and issues to them until the issue is resolved. By embracing the opportunity of working together looking at the most deep and pressing issues that tend to keep representing...to both the supervisee and supervisor...then both the supervisee and supervisor can metamorphose into more insightful and wise practitioners.

Reflection point

What three issues or problems tend to reoccur for you in your work? How have you avoided these opportunities and what supervision might you need to gain insight into why you draw these to you and what you have to learn from them?

Conclusion

At the heart of all therapeutic work the therapist needs to heal and know themselves. Whether as a supervisee or supervisor the potential to be healed and to know yourself is engaged by passionate supervision. It can appear daunting and while the map is hard to interpret or seems invisible until you have journeyed across the territory, others have been before you and you are not alone. However, there are two very different ways of journeying through our professional lives. One is with fear; fear of not being in control, of getting hurt or lost and of being wounded or judged. The other is with love; love of our patients and ourselves, love of the uncertainty, opportunity and unknown (see Chapter 10). These are not just different views of health, practice and therapy but fundamental differences in how we perceive our world and the awareness of who we are and what we are engaged in. There are times when either can be appropriate and serve us, but it is important for each of us to realize we have a choice either to avoid the unknown or welcome it. In the cauldron of our work we can either be consumed or metamorphose.

If individual therapeutic relationships are to be central to the caring professions then transformative, passionate supervision needs to be championed not just by supervisors and supervisees, but also by clients and patients, and the professional organizations that do so much to determine the context and culture in which supervision is provided. The wisdom gained from taking part in passionate supervision needs to be fed back into the bedrock on which practice is based and be reflected in the work and values of our professional organizations. The supervisees in passionate supervision today are the passionate supervisors of tomorrow. They provide the very 'life blood' of our practices and have earned the voice to guide our professions.

Introduction to Chapter 4

Sheila's focus is on the quality of looking we bring to supervision whether of the individual or the system. She reminds us that we can't look again at anything if we can't remember what happened in the first place, and we can't move on, make a shift, unless we know where we are now. Mindful supervision pays attention to what is happening and notices our tendencies to edit, censor and shape experience to fit preconceived ideas. Sheila sees supervision as a chance to perceive experience afresh.

When I asked Sheila what she most wanted the reader to gain from reading the chapter she said:

> Courage: In literally stopping for a breather, we can reconnect with that rage of the heart that gets us up every day to practise our helping and healing arts.
>
> In pausing myself to write this chapter, I've gained fresh insight into what moves me – and that's hardly a comfortable knowing. But it gets me back in touch with what's real, with what I know from experience, and that restores courage to stand ground and to act. And the action now comes from a more vulnerable and a more truthful place. And that is a powerful act. The invitation to you is to pause for breath and inquire within.

Chapter 4

Mindful Supervision
Sheila Ryan

Supervision as a quality of looking.

Caught up as we are in the need to be doing; to fix, recover and restore, supervision can be a space in which to just be.

Mindful supervision brings a quality of looking at practice without fear or favour – except of course we do fear and we do favour – and we can just be with that too.

In this chapter we see what a potent agent for change this quality of looking can be.

Supervision is located as a form of compassionate inquiry, a consciousness raising activity and a lifelong learning.

Daily practices to encourage this mindful approach are given. Stories from organizational, one-to-one and self-supervision show the quality in action.

Introduction

I am passionate about supervision. When I stop to look at what is really going on; with me, the client and the space in between, then practice becomes an everyday miracle. I wake up to the creativity, the innate competence and the compassion with which we are trying to relate to each other.

In this chapter we will see what a potent agent for change supervision can be, simply in its willingness to look and to stay with what's there. When we take a moment to pause, to rewind and replay the action we see more clearly what the matter is – and what we are already doing to make it better. In our desire for change we can miss the point: we don't notice that what we need is already there if we would only be still and listen for it, step back and let it come. Supervision can re-connect us with our experience, to what we knew before we censored, interpreted and changed it to fit this way and that.

But how do we to get in touch with that fresh encounter – literally re-member it? And before that, how do we even have our own experience in the first place?

Picture this: I am eating lunch while reading a book when my eyes wander to the clock and my mind to a thought about the next appointment and then on to something I've forgotten to do. What now is my experience of reading the book, let alone of tasting the food?

Presence

To have our experience in the first place it helps to be there at the time. When we are fully present it becomes much easier to recall that experience at will.

Before the Norwegian painter Edward Munch really looked at sunlight on water, it was conventionally painted as a light which streamed outward as it approached the shore. He could see that the beam he was looking at in fact shone in a more or less straight column from the sun on the horizon to the shore line. His being present to the beam upset a habitual way of seeing and enabled us to look anew. This is what supervision, as a mindful quality of looking, can do for our practice. It can interrupt a routine way of doing things and let us see it another way.

Mindfulness

We talk a lot about boundaries in practice. The only real boundary is to immerse ourselves in the here and now. The past and the future don't leak into the experience if we are truly present to it. Now we really do 'know' from experience. We can then go on to remember it, story it, map it and theorize about it. Then the doing is in Winnicott's words (1986 p.39): 'The doing that arises out of being'. Mindful supervision encourages us to base our actions upon our real embodied experience. It encourages us to make theories, maps and models for practice which are meaningful to us.

Peter Reason (1994) puts it like this:

> Knowing is more valid-richer, deeper, more true to life and more useful if these four ways of knowing are congruent with each other: If our knowing is grounded in our experience, expressed through our stories and images, understood through theories that make sense to us, and expressed in worthwhile action in our lives. (p.338)

For supervision to work as a space in which to learn more about our practice (Carroll 1999) we need to foster the voices of benign and interested inquiry. If we step back only to find the harsh critic in charge, then supervision becomes an inquisition to be avoided at all costs. And the cost to the practitioner of avoiding inquiry altogether can mean the loss of real and meaningful engagement with clients. If we can bring our own gentle enough voices to the task and make trustworthy enough relationships with others too in order to inquire into practice, then the fear of getting it wrong can drop away and return us to practice with compassion – literally with passion (Ryan 2004, p.44 and pp.169–170).

This mindful quality of looking belongs to ancient tradition. It is passed down to us for example as Vipassana meditation from South and South East Asia. Vipassana means to see things as they really are, insight or clear awareness (Gunaratana 1992).

Mindfulness finds a home in transpersonal approaches to healing and therapy and forms the explicit basis for many new initiatives in therapy including Acceptance and Commitment Therapy (ACT) (Hayes and Strosahl 2004). Hayes identifies fusion on the one hand (confusion of thoughts about reality with actual experience of reality) and emotional avoidance on the other, as the two main obstacles to being present to our experience. In response to these obstacles to being here, mindfulness training is a simple, effective, daily life saving practice for client and therapist as well as for daily life. That's what it is for me, a flawed and struggling daily practice, more often showing me my mindlessness and my mind chattering than it does any mastery of the mind. And yet the benefits still accrue. They are simply this: in becoming, even for a moment, more interested in than attached to a particular moment, more mindful of what is present, we find a freedom to move where before we may have felt quite stuck or unable to focus or heavily burdened by responsibility – literally unable to respond.

The practice of this mindful quality of looking, in the context of a relationship whose purpose is to inquire into practice in the helping and healing professions, is for me the art of supervision.

The breath is the simplest object we can turn our attention to in order to strengthen the habit of mindfulness. The effect of this simple and routine practice of focus on the breath is that I am more alive to the moment, more present, more in the 'here and now' (Stern 2004). These are all well-worn phrases used to describe that feeling of refreshment which comes with letting go of doing something all the time, let alone doing more than one thing at a time.

Through attention to the breath we can learn to watch changes in our physical sensations, feelings and perceptions. We learn to study our own mental activities and the fluctuations in consciousness itself. Focus on the breath, practised regularly, can mean we start to notice more and more of our own experience. It is a gentle technique that is also very thorough.

In the context of supervision, our intention to be more aware of what is happening is supported by mindfulness training. The rewards are incremental. With regular practice over time, mindfulness or awareness makes us more alive to experience. We 'wake up' as it were: we smell more acutely, we touch more fully and we really pay attention to what we feel. We learn to listen to our own thoughts without being caught up in them. Practice then becomes life-enhancing rather than a burden. We are filled not with worry and concern, but with curiosity. We feel compassion instead of frustration. Great benefits from such a simple practice! There are guides for mindfulness training at the end of the chapter.

Three stories

The three stories in this chapter are chosen to illustrate mindful supervision in action. They each turn upon the hand gesture and upon images newly created in the supervision. Both the gestures and the images have the power to re-create experience for the supervisees, to put them back in touch with themselves, and in so doing restore their power to move and to act.

The homeopath and teacher Rajan Sankaran (2001) follows both traditional wisdom and his own empirical research to identify the hand gesture as a reliable teller of the more elemental story in any interaction. Myths and fairy tales, archetypal images and dreams have always been a source of wisdom. We are a story-telling people. We make and remake the story of our lives. And for every story there needs to be a listener. And with each new listener the telling is changed. We are always making and remaking the story of our lives in relationship to each other.

This 'elemental story' (Ryan 2004, pp.40–42) is the one not yet told. It is forgotten or buried. It has been censored as too painful, fearful, wrong or inconsequential perhaps. And it holds the key to learning and to healing. It is waiting for the right kind of listener, the actively mindful listener. With the telling of the new story, the one more true to experience, comes the possibility of change and renewal. The elemental story is a vital one. It has the power to move us. It carries energy as shown to us through body language, art–play (Ryan 2004, p.57), image and metaphor. More usually we exchange our 'comfort stories,' those anecdotes with which we are familiar and with which we seek to map and to explain our lives thus far.

Here's a short story to illustrate something of the mindful quality of looking in action. It shows how a new insight might be achieved in a supervisory relationship.

Sitting on my hands: A doctor becomes a supervisor

As an external supervisor of final examination interviews for a supervision diploma in Czech Republic (Iron Mill Institute UK), I was working with a translator into English. In one interview, fatigued by the effort of listening to the translator as well as observing the interaction, I decided to tune out the whispered words. This is what happens:

I begin to release the tension in me caused by the effort of concentrating on the translator by first turning my attention to my own breath. I find as usual that it both relaxes and 'wakes me up'.

Now the incomprehensible triad of candidate and two examiners, talking and gesticulating away in Czech, seems literally to slow down in front of me. I no longer look at them with a 'hard eyed' concentration as I strain to understand. A small smile begins to soften the edges of my mouth and I notice I am breathing slow and easy. My legs uncross themselves where before they had been wound round each other. I couldn't say whether what happens next also happened before in this examination, but now I notice that the candidate stops waving her hands about as she talks and sits on them instead. Since this is about the only thing I notice during the viva, at the end I ask if sitting on her hands is significant to her in any way. (I explain that 'sitting on hands' is a phrase we use in English to describe doing nothing.) Her hand now flies to her mouth. She says:

> This is my dilemma as a supervisor. I am a doctor and am used to being the one to give the medicines. It is hard for me to 'sit on my hands' as a supervisor and allow the supervisee to prescribe. I did not notice that I literally sat on my hands during this presentation and I did not discuss this aspect of the supervision during the viva although actually it is the hardest part of being a supervisor for me.

The hand gesture tells her story simply and beautifully and I may have missed it if I had not become, through focus on my own breath, more present to the moment. In offering the observation to the candidate, she then decides on the value to her of the observation. Between us we identify a core issue for her in her story of becoming a supervisor.

PARADOX

Supervision paradoxically, since it is a place to think about experience in practice (Shipton 1997), is itself an experience.

It is also a paradox that supervision shifts a situation simply by accepting the way it is, walking all around it as it were, looking at it this way and that, trying it out this way and that, just playing at it, the way children play; with complete attention, wholeheartedly, lost in worlds.

The practice of mindfulness, paying attention, 'waking up' (Balint 1959) to what is happening, encourages us to tell it another way. It can lead us through the enchantment, the spell practice can put us under, where we can no longer see what is happening because we are a part of the story ourselves and yet under the illusion that we are separate from it, watching without participation.

Here is a story from supervision of an organization. The role of the independent supervisor, as an outsider to the organization, is to be free to explore the nature and characteristics of that culture and to help the participants in it to see the part they play and the freedom they may or may not have to contribute to maintaining or changing it. Of course, as the supervisor working with the organization, I 'catch' the culture too…

A college changes hands

I am asked by a college principal to facilitate a management team meeting, the first since a change in ownership of the college. I am told in preparation that there are 'dark mutterings abroad' about whom the new management would cast off and what unwelcome changes there might be.

The whole team, including the Principal, are willing to share this vulnerable time with an outsider. This already tells me something about the culture: the college values and supports an open approach to conflict. There is possibility here then to work with fear and loss. (Organizations which support a culture of blame and shame will not tend to open their doors readily to an independent supervisor who may well be feared as a critical rather than a compassionate inquirer.)

It is the supervisor's task here to initiate and hold this spirit of compassionate inquiry. This team meeting starts with an initial round of introductions and the instruction to sit quietly and be with the breath. After a few minutes, the group is guided to focus on any tension held in the body. The suggestion is made to breathe into that tension. (This is a short cut to getting in touch with ourselves and cutting through the 'comfort stories' into experience of the present moment.) After this, the round begins Quaker style, with each person introducing themselves anew as and when they are moved to speak. This is what happens:

From stillness in the room supported by the initial quiet attention to the breath, metaphors for the transition period begin spontaneously to emerge. One person tells of being an 'old hand' and the difficulty of learning new ways. Another picks this up with a feeling of the loss of 'a safe pair of hands' with the departure of the old college principal. Another team member urges 'all hands on deck' to make a fresh start. Gradually a collective imagery emerges. Encouraged now to follow the images into story, the team begins to share the difficult feelings of loss and of fear of the future. Through story they seem to take bolder steps into the unknown and to risk sharing their vulnerabilities.

> We don't have to cling to everything we had before in the old country. Like emigrants, we can take on board with us only what we value, and that we can each carry.

> Can I bear to let go of that life in the old country? Perhaps I don't want to come on board at all.

> We are setting sail on an adventure. We don't yet know who the captain is but we do know each other and we're a good crew.

> We can work together, all hands on deck, to make sure we get across safely.
>
> I can spy the land ahead but I can't make out all the contours. I can't see yet where we can safely land but that will get clearer as we get closer.

Storying together creates an 'aesthetic distance' (Jennings 1998, p.115). This enables us to stay with an experience without becoming engulfed by it – it contains a supervisory quality of looking – being in it and seeing ourselves in it. The distance is not an emotional coldness but rather a transcendence created by an artistic, metaphorical experience.

In this way, vulnerabilities are expressed without blame. Images are shared to sustain the team in an insecure time of change. The metaphors the team produces have the power to transform individual fears and worries into a collective story of endings, new beginnings, endeavour and adventure.

I came away with a real sense of loss after this intensive day together. I wanted for a moment there to be an ongoing part of this adventure and not just an outsider invited in for the day. I had 'caught' the story of loss in not being on board for the journey (parallel process; see Hawkins and Shohet 2006). I also came away with the image of supervisor as a 'safe pair of hands' in a moment of transition when the college is rocked by this handing over from one Principal to another. I left finally with an image of watching from the shore, a ship well crewed, anchors away, heading out into the open ocean.

THE 13TH FAIRY

Supervision does not accept what is presented at face value. It is looking with interest into all that is there and includes the discarded, the discounted and the disgraced.

In folklore, a common feature of the fairies is the use of magic to disguise appearance. Fairy gold is notoriously unreliable, appearing as gold when paid, but soon thereafter revealing itself to be leaves, or gingerbread cakes, or a variety of other (useless) things.

Supervision is about waking up to the enchantment we are under. Fairy ointment in the old myths, when put on the eyes, allows us to see how things really are. Likewise, supervision brings to light the elements we have edited out of our stories deeming them too dangerous to include, too awkward, too embarrassing, too out of place, too uncomfortable, too trivial, too useless, too frightening.

Supervision attempts the dangerous enterprise of bringing to light the gold thus disguised in the muck and miry old crone's rags. It invites the unwelcome stranger in, the 13th fairy. Gives it houseroom. Strives to make its acquaintance. Asks it to rest awhile.

'Take off your hat, come in, sit down, and bide awhile.'

Here's a little of my own story about how I come to be so passionate about supervision – is it a 'comfort' story I know already or is there fresh insight to be found in this telling?

Second hand

The dark holds terror. What is more frightening to me than the dark, however, is not knowing what it hides. I must screw up my courage and peer in if ever so cautiously and always ready to run. I must fetch whatever is down there up into the light. I need to risk it because not doing so is worse, far worse. If I don't then my imagination runs a riot of fears. And worse still: if I don't look, nothing really happens. Nothing real happens. It's as if my own life is being lived second hand.

To tell it as story, it is like a ship in the dark without satellite navigation, nosing along in a sea of icebergs, a weak lantern swinging over the bow; the night watch looks out to see those ghostly shapes, which unseen in the night, might just become silent ship wreckers.

As a child I found getting to sleep difficult. I didn't know how to do it. I had the idea that I needed to stay awake – to be the night watcher. Later on, as I sought cures for what became a crippling insomnia, I found healing through the breath. I began to sleep and then to remember, at first in dreams, experiences that made sense of the need I had to stay awake. Insomnia itself wasn't the problem. It was my childish attempt to respond to a deeper issue, a perceived lack of safety. I needed to stay alert.

Staying alert became consciousness raising in the women's movement of the 1970s. We told our own stories and empathized with each others'. In this way personal struggles became shared histories. 'The personal is political', we said then. And from this new minted identity as women, movement grows and with it my own sense of self.

Later on again as a student of homeopathy, now in the 1980s, I set about forming what we would come to call peer supervision groups. Here we can share our experience of practice in a mutually supportive and challenging environment as we had once before in the consciousness raising groups.

I thought at first that this need to share experience of practice was because I was a new practitioner. Twenty-five years on I meet still in different peer supervision groups with practitioners who are decidedly long in the tooth, who are teachers and supervisors themselves. And we still say things like: 'I am bringing shame today' and 'Some days I am confident in what I do and other days I'm a fraud.'

After two decades or so we can still come fresh to the task of meeting a new client. There are few expert routines in our expertise. Instead, competent clinical judgments are born, as daily miracles, out of personal vulnerability to new experience.

In telling the story here I see anew that what we present as the problem is in fact the solution to another, more deeply buried issue. The presenting problem is the gift the 13th fairy brings: insomnia is seen here to be a response to fear of falling asleep in an unsafe place. It sets me on a path of consciousness raising and it is therefore no surprise I should be engaged in supervision – the act of waking up to what happens in practice.

The doctor wakes up to her conflict between 'doing' and 'being' in noticing she is sitting on her hands.

The college team present fear of 'who will be cast off' only to find that casting off is exactly what they need to do.

Passionate supervision in action

Gesture, metaphor, poetry, story and song have transformative power (for more on using creative methods in supervision see Chapters 7 and 8): supervision as a re-creation of worlds. In writing and re-writing our stories of practice, checking them out against experience, testing them up against theory, we see the presenting issues in new lights and so bring new possibilities for acceptance, movement and change. A working knowledge of archetype, myth and fairy tale and a willingness to follow gesture and metaphor as moving lines can bring rich insight into any interaction.

Supervision, which employs this mindful quality of looking, is dynamic in that it has the power to move us on as well as to reveal meaning to us: mindfulness as a way of life, a daily practice, not a perfect. A mindful supervision of the helping professions can help us to stay open to experience in all its wonderful and perplexing complexity. In getting back in touch with the full experience we are free to respond, with creativity, to each fresh encounter.

A three-step guide to mindfulness training

These exercises are based on the teachings of Thich N'hat Hanh.

Focus on the breath 1

Sit down comfortably. Make some contact with the floor or ground either by sitting on a chair with your feet planted or by sitting on the ground.

Now simply bring awareness to your breath. Just that. Notice your breath as you inhale and exhale. Notice your mind wandering from the task and notice yourself bringing your mind back to the task of being mindful of your breath. Begin with three minutes and with practice extend the time.

Focus on the breath 2

As for exercise 1. Now count your 'in' breath. Don't try to alter it, just count it. For example say 'in 2, 3, 4, 5'; 'out 2, 3, 4, 5, 6, 7'. You may have even 'in' and 'out' breaths or shorter 'in' and longer 'out' breaths. It doesn't matter. Just count the breaths in and out.

What you may notice is that as you practise this, your breathing does quite naturally deepen and slow down. You may put a hand on your abdomen and feel the breath rise and fall. You may notice instead that your breath is shallow and tight and located somewhere above your solar plexus especially to begin with. With practice it will slow and lengthen and deepen and you will experience the rise and fall of your abdomen.

At this point, when you can easily tune into your abdominal breathing, the practice becomes a lifesaver. Whenever you are caught up in a reaction in life, practice or supervision, you now have the facility to return to the breath for a moment. This pause and return to yourself brings calm and a more freely given response in place of a button pushed, knee jerk reaction.

Focus on the breath 3

As for exercise 2. Now stand up. Find a space to walk in. Outside in nature is good of course. It will support your practice. A busy street and a cluttered room are also suitable, as they will test your ability to stay focused.

The practice both supports and tests you. As you step, step mindfully. Be aware of your foot lifting and stepping on to the ground, making contact. For every step, you count 1 in time with your breath. Step 1 is in breath 1, and step 2 is in breath 2, etc. Stepping with each count of your breath in and out.

You can also step slowly and make the first step one full in breath and the second a full out breath (Nguyen Anh-Huong and Thich N'hat Hanh 2006).

In this way, mindfulness practice can happen when you are sitting and when you are walking. At any time of the day we can tune into the breath and into mindfulness of stepping in time with the breath.

References

Balint, M. (1959) *Thrills and Regressions*. London: Hogarth Press.

Carroll, M. (1999) 'Training in the tasks of supervision.' In E. Holloway and M. Carroll (1999) *Training Counselling Supervisors*. London: Sage.

Gunaratana, B.H. (1992) *Mindfulness in Plain English*. Somerville, MA: Wisdom Publications.

Hawkins, P. and Shohet, R. (2006) *Supervision in the Helping Professions*, pp.93–5. Oxford: OUP.

Hayes, S. and Strosahl, K. (eds) (2004) *A Practical Guide to Acceptance and Commitment Therapy*. New York: Springer.

Jennings, S. (1998) 'Ariadne's ball of thread.' In *Introduction to Drama Therapy, Theatre and Healing*. London: Jessica Kingsley Publishers.

Nguyen Anh-Huong and Thich N'hat Hanh (2006) *Walking Meditation*. Boulder, CO: Sounds True.

Reason, P. (1994) 'Three approaches to participative inquiry.' In N.K. Denzin and Y.S. Lincoln (eds) *Handbook of Qualitative Research,* pp.324–339. Thousand Oaks, CA: Sage.

Ryan, S. (2004) *Vital Practice Stories from the Healing Arts: The Homeopathic and Supervisory Way.* Portland, OR: Sea Change.

Sankaran, R. (2001) *An Insight into Plants Vol. 1.* Mumbai: Homeopathic Medical Publishers.

Shipton, G. (ed.) (1997) *Supervision of Psychotherapy and Counselling – Making a Place to Think.* Oxford: OUP.

Stern, D. (2004) *The Present Moment in Psychotherapy and Everyday Life.* New York: Norton.

Winnicot, D.W. (1986) 'Living creatively.' In Winnicott, D.W. *Home Is Where We Start From: Essays by a Psychoanalyst.* New York: W.W. Norton.

Introduction to Chapter 5

Joan's chapter also focuses on the here and now in the room and specifically looks at the supervisory relationship, which she sees as a vessel for transformation. What stands out for me is her ability to see many levels simultaneously and how she can weave all these levels into her relationships with supervisees, helping them to see how what is happening in the room can mirror what is going on outside the room.

When I asked Joan what she most wanted the reader to gain from reading her chapter, she replied:

> What I most want the reader to gain from reading the chapter is that having a passionate supervision relationship for one's employment, whatever it is, provides a space for a joyful creative work life and a unique opportunity for soul work, heartfelt support, challenge, and cosmic humour. Having just written this, the following week, I was leaving the building where I had been running a long-term monthly supervision group when a member stopped me and said she wanted me to know that what happened in the group not only helped them in their work but also in the rest of their lives.

Chapter 5

The Supervisory Relationship: A Lifelong Calling

Joan Wilmot

In this chapter I am trying to explain the inexplicable. I see supervision as a hologram in which each moment contains everything that needs to be embodied, felt and known. The different worlds of the client, supervisee, supervisor and the outside world are simultaneously mirroring and co-creating each other. Supervision offers us the opportunity to become present to that moment of awareness so that the wound, disturbance or disconnection that seems to be breaking us and everything apart is instead the road back home.

> The part that knows does not speak and the part that speaks does not know. (Lao Tzu)

Those words reflect some of how I feel on moving from being a supervisor to writing about it, and especially trying to capture the nature of the supervisory relationship. It is probably because the nature of focusing on anything is paradoxical. It both illuminates, inhibits and also changes the process. There is the old joke about the centipede moving gracefully across the ground until someone asks him how he moves with so many legs, at which point he promptly falls over. And that is it. We reflect on our work in supervision so that we can become more graceful, more adept, more competent, more able, and yet the real value may be in the inglorious, clumsy, embarrassing falling over which offers potential freedom from old paradigms and beliefs.

So what happens when I sit down to supervise? What is that state of heightened awareness in which I listen? The ears of the cells of my body lean into the story that the supervisee is telling about the clients, about themselves. I go into the depth, the breadth, the observation, the sensation, the dream, the anything and everything and the nothing. I do not dismiss anything, anything that I think, feel, smell, hear. If I get bored I see what that may be telling me, if I drift off out of the room I ask myself where did I go, when did I go and when did I come back? I notice how my energy moves in my body. Sometimes I have felt so tired that it is as if I am falling into an abyss, and like in John Keats's *Ode to a Nightingale*, 'Lethe-wards had sunk'. Other times I am highly alert, aware of the different levels simultaneously; and yet there is still so much that I miss, am blind to. I am both carried along into the state, or the thought, or the feeling and at the same time I am observing it, gathering the gifts, the silver, the gold, the lead, like the caskets in Shakespeare's 'Merchant of Venice', placing them carefully on the metaphorical shelves of the mind, sifting through and watching all this weave itself into a thought, a sentence, an illumination of the client, the supervisee, their relationship. I watch as if for the first time and at the same time the familiar parallels in the room between me and them, them and their client, and the archetypes of human life are appearing in the oddest places, and in the strangest behaviour.

Being intensely engaged in relationship with another person is one of the greatest joys of being human (De Quincey 2000). This is how I supervise and why I supervise and will continue to do so I imagine for the rest of my life.

The first supervisory relationship

When did I first experience myself as supervisor? A part of
me that reflected on me, my feelings, my behaviour, my
relationship with others; family, friends, neighbours, school,
my immediate neighbourhood, my culture; hard to know
when this type of consciousness arises in us; when one part of
us reflects on another part of us. Do we do it because it is
inevitable, like moving from crawling to walking? And/or do
we do it as the result of something that interrupts us, hurts us,
confuses us and we develop reflection to ease the anguish, find
a way of being in control again? Or do we do it because we are
drawn towards learning as an end in itself and this ability to
reflect seems to nourish the learning? What does seem clear is
that this process of supervision, which I have been passionately
engaged in all my adult life, started way before my paid work.

Another memory as a child, maybe around the age of eight
or nine, is of reading about someone who drowned in a river
even though there were several people on the banks nearby. I
realized that we can become paralysed and fall 'asleep' and that
one needs to practise techniques for staying 'awake', otherwise
I could be the one standing on the bank of life, frozen,
unavailable to another or myself. So whom did I want to 'save'?
Myself without doubt, and the others who are both themselves
and also those parts of myself that I am still addicted to fixing
and resistant to simply loving. Harold Searles (1975) said that
as well as wanting to heal ourselves we come to heal our
parents, and if we go into therapy, our therapist. So mutual
healing is a very necessary human need. A need that we are
intensely involved with, until we arrive and know that there
was never anything to heal. A journey, as Robin Shohet writes
in Chapter 10, from fear to love or from story to no story.

So it seems that the first remembered or conscious
supervisory relationship I had was with myself. And then I

wonder if it were good or bad, relaxed or tense, critical or compassionate. And did we have a supervisory alliance? Were we on the same side and whose side might that be? Who and how did we decide? Did we have shared goals and did we ever contract? And so far as I can see it was all of these and more. So one could wonder if an external supervisory relationship, whether we are supervisor or supervisee, would be most coloured by our original relationship with ourself; the self that arrived in the world and rapidly shaped itself through its experiences of the world. Coupled with this is the sense it made of its experiences, and the mirrors to itself that it received from its parents and those around it. And all this happens before the development of language that both offers us sense making, meaning and at the same time limits and fixes us.

And then I was the eldest girl responsible for my younger sister and brother, so they were my first visible supervisees.

The second supervisory relationship

So maybe it was also a relief when I first came to supervision as a supervisee; a chance to do what I had been doing internally with myself externally with someone else who, at least for the duration of the session, was as interested in me as I was? And also a persecution; are they going to be as angry and critical of me as I am and bully me and harangue me in the way I do myself; are they going to shame or humiliate me by drawing attention to parts of myself that I do not appear to know despite the close monitoring that I have invested in all these years prior to meeting this stranger on the other side of the carefully arranged space between us?

So these stories of relationship are travelling with us, both supervisor and supervisee, before even the first meeting is arranged. I am reminded of how in our supervision training we do a contracting exercise where we divide the group into 'supervisee group' and 'supervisor group' and ask each group what their hopes and fears are for the relationship. Each time we discover the same hopes and fears were felt in both groups, fear of being attacked, rejected or criticized and hopes of being appreciated, valued, and effective. My story of relationship also points to other factors, in particular the supervisory alliance; do we trust or do we make enemy images of the other?

Early on in my career I was upset with another staff member for not supporting me. I was seeing her as an enemy. In supervision my supervisor asked me, 'When did you first walk out on yourself?' I was startled at the question but found myself giving the answer, 'Two years old'. I realized that it was not the staff member who was the problem; they had not walked out on me, failed to support me. I was the one that had done that. So the exquisite paradox of supervision that never ceases to engage me is the dance of opposites; the truth is usually the opposite of what I believed. The so called 'bad' experience leads to the light, the light to the darkness; the detail leads to the bigger picture; the bigger picture is illuminated by the specific; the breakdown becomes the breakthrough and everything, but everything is relevant and grist to the mill. So my supervisor in being able to help me stay with the paradox of the story of being unsupported by the other enabled me to see the story of my 'abandonment' in a different light. I did not have an issue with the staff member. It was I who had created the separation, the story of abandonment. They had done what they had done; it was my reaction to their action that was the difficulty. I had gone into, you could say 'got off' on, my story of being a victim and being left and was no longer in the present.

Story and no story

I am entranced by the paradox of story and no story. For some years now I have been very engaged with the work of Byron Kathleen Mitchell, known as Byron Katie (2002), who 'woke up' one day from her rage and depression. She saw that everything, but everything that she had ever believed was not true. She describes this experience as, ' "it" was laughing, the only thing that existed was awareness' (p.xii) and she felt absolute delight. And there was no thought. She devised a method of investigating our stories to see if we can really know that they are true; these four questions:

1.   Is it true?

2.   Can you really know it's true?

3.   How do you react when you believe the thought (the story)?

4.   Who would you be without the thought?

The final step is the 'turn around' (similar to owning projections), inquiring into the stories that bring us so much stress. In her seeing there is no story, and at the same time inquiring into the truth or not of the story, she asks with loving compassion, 'Who would you be without your story?' (p.6) Then the 'box breaks' (Jochen Encke, Chapter 1) and the spell dissolves. So that is what it feels like to me being in a supervisory relationship. The supervisee and I focus intently on the client's story, the supervisee's story of the client, and in being present to the story there is a shift, or what Bert Hellinger (2006) calls a fleeting moment of truth when the soul is engaged. Many people have experienced that after such a shift in the session, the resulting intervention that the supervisee decides to make in the next session is not needed. The client has already moved.

For the last eight years I have been a member of Playback Theatre, a form of improvisation drama, in which members of the audience are invited to share moments or incidents from their everyday life and have them played back by the actors. The actors are not trying to interpret the story. Instead they are entering into the story and playing it back to the 'teller' in its essential essence so that in this process the 'teller', in watching it, may be released from his or her story. When this happens there is the 'ah ha moment' (see Chapter 3) for 'the teller', the freedom from the pain and problem of the story, a movement into truth and awareness, a sense of commonality and connectedness with the human race.

As I write, an example of that process presents itself, in which my supervisee, Joyce, and I go behind the known and oft repeated story of her client. We are focused on her client, James, and his painful early childhood, a childhood that started with a traumatic birth where there appears to have been a lack of security, continuity, or holding. We are in a sense giving him that attention his life did not appear to have. We are becoming more and more present as Joyce speaks and the attention comes from the ground that we have gardened together over our 12 years of monthly supervision sessions. I pare away the 'story' part of the story so that we begin to see him not just as his story of him, or our story of him. Then from our doing that Joyce remarks that she just realized what his job is. 'He is a health and safety officer,' she says. At that moment we see the opposite of the 'painful' story. Whereas before we had seen the lack; we see the continuity, the security and the holding; his whole life from now to then is a seamless whole and we experience that wholeness as laughter. It was as if the life force of his life came through at that moment and not just the pain. That painful story was but one part of him and now there is another part, the ever-changing present and presentness of his essence as we talk about him. We have moved from pathology to core.

Containing anxiety

One of the primary tasks of supervision is the containment of anxiety, our own, the clients', the supervisees' and all those in the wider system; from immediate family to other stakeholders such as the health service, social services and society itself. In fact Gilbert and Evans (2000) write that they have become 'meticulously careful about any action that is based on vague information and paranoid fantasies'. In other words they can see how the story creates and feeds on itself because of anxiety. So in the end one is not dealing with the original event but the anxiety around the stories of the event.

My co-trainer and I had first-hand experience of this when we were running a supervision course in London at the time of the July 2005 bombings. Containing the anxiety around a very real event coupled with a constant flow of television coverage in the reception area of the building where we were working, along with the fantasies engendered by not being able to get through on that supposedly instant communication technology, the mobile phone, was a here and now living of that premise. We had to walk our talk; bear with the anxiety, our own and the participants', neither splitting off from it nor ceding to it and to find and stay with what was our authentic business at that time.

What was the business we had contracted to do, and were the other options that had now presented, e.g. going home early, stopping the course, more real than the original intention we had consciously formed at the beginning of our three days together? Were the feelings running through us authentic and leading to right action right now, or were they a dream or nightmare that we were seducing ourselves into? Were we addicted to fear and adrenalin and could therefore our actions feed our fear culture both in and outside ourselves? How could we best serve in that seemingly high drama scenario that threatened to sweep us away before we found that still place, the essential core of supervision? We were also having to challenge some of the core beliefs of the society we live in about what keeps us safe, with everybody wanting to know where everybody in their family and friends were.

Barry Mason (1993) says that people 'in periods of great stress' want to find a position of what he calls 'safe certainty'. In this case it was wanting to get home immediately or have phone contact rather than carry on with the training which was part of their future of becoming a supervisor. In other cases such as child protection cases where there has been loss of life, it is drawing up contracts which cover everything in an attempt to provide for every possibility. Supervision then if we can hold our nerve offers a container where we can rest in uncertainty.

Supervision as cornerstone of work

Supervision is a wonderful process in that its purpose is to attend to our work and our work life. I believe it is unique because its focus *is* work and because of the unique place of work in our psyches. I think everyone's work, whatever kind of work it is, without exception, benefits from having the time regularly to reflect on it with someone they respect who is enthusiastic, committed and experienced.

When two commentators were discussing Roger Federer during his finals match at Wimbledon in 2005 one of them remarked that he had chosen Roach to be his coach. As Federer was self-taught and the general opinion was that his game was so excellent that there was nothing to improve, they were wondering why he would be taking on a coach. One of the commentators said he knew that Federer 'had a lot of respect for Roachy'.

And work as cornerstone of life

Peter Caddy, one of the founders of the Findhorn Community, in North East Scotland, where I currently live, believed that 'Work is Love in Action'. An Australian study found that what most improved low self-esteem was getting back to work. Work is a very central part of our lives; we expend much time and energy in doing it, thinking about it, looking for it if we are not in work, evaluating ourselves in relation to our success or failure at it. We wonder as children 'What am I going to be when I grow up!' It is one of the ways we embody who we are and how we engage with our world. It meets our need for meaning. It is how we give expression to our inner life in our outer life, the journey from private to public. So meaningful work is vital to us and our well-being; in it we can play and create and learn, and not being right at work saps our life force. So I appreciate in supervision the opportunity, the gift of the other in coming to meet with me, to turn the potential stress and burn out around so that the supervisee re-finds their joy either in the work they are in or finds the work that brings them joy.

Given work plays such an essential part in our financial, emotional and spiritual life I enjoy how supervision/reflective practice provides a space where we can give attention to our work selves. A definition I heard recently is that any work or occupation is made up of ritual, intention and relationship. It does not matter whether we are working as a brain surgeon, a road sweeper or a therapist. The ritual is the task and the training we have undertaken for that task, the intention is how we approach our work, our commitment to it and then the third component is the relationship we have to it, the people we meet at work and ourselves.

The whole of our life patterns and life issues seem to turn up in work and are consequently brought to supervision. Freud said that our dreams are the royal road to the unconscious, but I think from being a supervisor and supervisee for the last 35 years that work provides this high road. It is amazing how work colleagues, the management or the client group, be they children if you are a teacher, patients if you are a doctor, or the general public if you work in shops, etc. can press our buttons. They turn up on cue to be mirrors of those parts of ourselves that we thought we did not have or if we did know we had we thought we had under control! Without a place such as a regular supervisory relationship provides to reflect on these crucial and core issues, we may miss an opportunity for the soul work that they offer, the chance to face our fears and enter a deeper intimate connection with ourselves and with the world around us. The means for doing this that supervision provides is the contract established between the supervisor and the supervisee that allows them to be open and explicit with each other with what needs to be attended to in the service of the work. The beauty of the supervision process and the supervisory relationship is that the quality of listening and presence there brings everything into alignment so that everyone is served.

Here and now and relationship

I value the immediacy of relationship in the here and now and permission to comment on it; permission to be curious; permission to slow everything down; to relish the richness of the ordinary and extraordinary all in one breath. And do I give myself permission? Oh yes! Sometime into my career I came across a quote credited to Laura Perls, Gestalt therapist, that the art of therapy is, 'to make the implicit explicit and state the obvious'. The same is true for supervision. This for me sums up my belief and my style. Having been brought up to stay out of the present and in particular commenting on it, what a joy that what often serves most in supervision is to do just that. As Yalom (2001) put it: 'Commentary on the here-and-now is a unique aspect of the therapeutic relationship. There are few human situations in which we are permitted, let alone *encouraged*, to comment upon the behaviour of the other.' When appropriate, we also make our own process equally available and transparent. 'It feels liberating, even exhilarating. But it also feels risky, since we are not accustomed to giving and receiving feedback.' So Yalom models commenting on his relationship with the client with such interventions as 'Let's take a minute to look at how you and I are doing today.' Or, 'Any feeling about how we are working or relating?' Or, 'Before we stop, shall we take a look at what's going on in this space between us?' I also hear Yalom's words echoing in my ears about 'the here and now – use it, use it, use it'.

As I write this I remember a moment of self-supervision with a client who was talking about an unfair situation at work where she was not allowed into certain meetings. While exploring this with her, I wondered if it were happening now between her and me. I could not see it. I felt we had a good working alliance. She was engaged with the therapy and seemed to be benefiting, but when the thought persisted I decided to ask her if there were anything unfair here and now between us. At which point she sat bolt upright and with more energy than she had prior to this said, 'Oh, yes! It is unfair that you know all about me and I know nothing about you.' So the issues of rank and privilege that we were looking at out there were now in the room. This aspect of the work, parallel process (a process in which what happens in one situation or relationship is repeated in another), is one of the aspects of the work that particularly excites me.

Parallel process

A recent example comes to mind. A relatively new supervisee rang me three days before her supervision session to ask if she could arrange a 15-minute phone session later in the day to discuss a client. I was hesitant, as my experience is that when we break the usual container, however useful the content, there can be something lost in terms of a lived learning through the process. When the supervisee said it was a boundary issue I was even more aware of that choice. It turned out that the client wanted to meet outside of the scheduled session. The supervisee wanted to say 'no' but was anxious that the client would feel abandoned, unsupported and angry. I suggested to the supervisee that we are in parallel process, that of setting a boundary. I was in her role of wanting to say 'no' and she was in the role of her client making the request. Instead of offering strategies for working with the client, I suggested to her that I might support her more with this issue by modelling saying 'no' to the extra time and giving her that experience. She said she felt unsupported by me and angry, just what she had feared from the client. I listened to her distress and again at her request shared my thinking. She did not seem satisfied then, but we finished our mini-session after the 15 minutes. She did not refer to it at the beginning of our session, but when I asked her about it she said she had thought about it, had understood the parallel, and most importantly had 'survived'. In fact this was part of the development of a more robust relationship between us in the first few months of our working together.

It seems to me that using the here and now and parallel process is often to do with timing, intention and relationship. Comment on the here and now and the parallel process too soon and we can lose the supervisee; they can feel overly challenged and unsupported and we can get into an ongoing power struggle, but leave it too long and we can also lose the supervisee, by going out of connection. By that I mean if we are always focusing on the out there, always talking about the clients and how, for example, they may be difficult to engage with, and never check out if this could be also true between ourselves and the supervisee, the vitality goes out of the relationship. However, before we become too anxious about commenting on the here and now or the parallel process, and doing it at the right time and in the right way, or in any other way needing to be a good supervisor and getting it right, we can also learn to trust the process. Life is very generous and gives us our lessons patiently and repeatedly until we can 'get it', as happened in the above example with my supervisee.

Paradox and not knowing

It is a lovely reminder not to become too attached to getting it right or taking the whole process so personally. I remember listening to Nina Coltart talking about her work as a psychoanalyst and how we can never know what works with our clients. In the times she received feedback from her clients after the therapy had finished, what they told her had helped them was either something she did not remember or was something that she had thought of as a mistake. They never ever referred to something that she had thought of as her best work. I enjoyed the way she was amused at herself and for her humility about it. Recently in a training course I was running we did tag supervision in which seven different supervisors in quite rapid succession offered seven different interventions to a supervisee who remained the same throughout the exercise. She said it was fabulous, all their interventions were useful and what she appreciated most from everyone was the quality of their attention.

So, in supervision as in life, we can never know how our interventions will be experienced; we could be having one experience and the person opposite could be having another. The Harvard Negotiation Project (1999) has encapsulated this notion in a very elegant and simple model of 'intent' and 'impact'. In my making an intervention only I can know my intent and only the receiver of my intervention can know its impact. Sometimes these are one and the same, but when they are not this seeming mismatch can offer an opportunity for new learning if we allow our curiosity rather than our hurt to invite us into exploring this mismatch. Gilbert and Evans (2000) write about these 'empathic failures' (Kohut 1984).

> An exploration of such miscommunications or discord lie at the heart of our approach to supervision of psychotherapy. We see that it is only through attending carefully to the times when we reach a person and the occasions that we 'miss' that person that we can truly learn to communicate effectively… Careful attention to communication at this microscopic level will lay the foundations for a firmly based relationship that is able to tolerate conflicts and disagreements and provide a container for growth and change.

Another aspect of paradox that interests me is the experience of committing to one truth and the opposite presenting itself. I have noticed this paradox particularly in the last two supervision trainings I have run. In the developing dialogue that has emerged in the group, in the moment when one person in the group has grasped a truth about supervision or about being a supervisor or supervisee, the opposite truth emerges. One member of the group talked about when they had held a very firm time boundary and how useful that had been. The group nodded in agreement and then almost immediately another group member recalled a time when they had allowed a client to run over and how beneficial that had been. Again the group nodded as they acknowledged the authenticity of that experience. So when the concept of 'one mind' can be understood we begin to work as one mind to hold the different and sometimes seemingly opposite levels, and that is one of the aspects of supervision that I just love; the different levels happening simultaneously and for a moment the language and the context to express it. For moments the group is able to be both individual and collective and to be in service to the truth, consciousness, love, relationship. It is true dialogue, which is engaging the soul, the mind, the body and the heart. We are indeed, in the words of the poet John Milton, in his epic poem, 'Paradise Lost' and used by Nina Coltart (1992) as the title of one of her books, *Slouching towards Bethlehem*.

So there we have it, the paradoxical nature of the whole business, engaging in my business, your business and our business to get to another person's business; immersing ourselves in story to get to no story; attempting to understand/control the world by attention and insight and in the very doing of this the transformation; the surrender that can emerge from its very opposite; and the continuum of love and fear, shame and authority as we focus on the practical desire to do a better job.

Systemic thinking and field theory

One of my passions is the form of dialogue that one can have in supervision, a conversation between two or more people in which the exploration of meaning between them is more important than one being 'right'. To me supervision gives me access to the bigger picture. As Rumi says, 'The field beyond right and wrong, I'll meet you there.' I love that process of taking the blame out of the frame, when the truth, the 'isness', is so much more nourishing than the right/wrong with which we humans have been trying to nourish ourselves. It happens in one-to-one supervision and in group supervision. A member of the group presents their team or organization and we look at the whole system. As we set up a living sculpture in which the group supervisee chooses members of the group to represent the different roles and aspects of the organization/system that we want to explore, the bigger picture begins to emerge. It becomes easier and easier to see how the whole system is co-creating the situation; everyone is interconnected and has some responsibility for what is happening, and everyone is always doing the best they can. We become more interested in becoming deeply present to what is, than judging it.

I enjoy the practical, poetic, paralleling, paradox and presentness of supervision. I am passionately interested in how the relationship out of the room, whether it is with a client or an organization, appears in the relationship in the room and as the two people in the room become present to themselves and each other, it is illuminated and changed, and vice versa and that this happens on many levels like ripples on a pond into which a stone has been dropped. The microcosm is the macrocosm, the container and the contained.

Lynne McTaggart (2003) describes it as an energy field, the Zero Point Field, that connects everything in the universe, and we ourselves are part of this vast dynamic web of energy exchange.

I find this concept particularly useful in one-to-one supervision, especially at times when the supervisee and I may become 'stuck', or get into conflict or each find the other 'difficult' or 'insensitive'. Instead of labelling each of us, we can notice that there is stuckness or insensitivity in the room in the space between us. It belongs to both of us. An example occurred this week with a long-term supervisee. We took on different positions in relation to what needed to be the focus of the work with her client and my supervisee was angry with me. After we had tussled for several minutes, we had the breakthrough and her ongoing work with her client became clear. She said how much she valued our long-term relationship which had allowed her to stay that angry with me and at the same time to know that we were both working together, co-creating and occupying two different positions as a way of deepening the connection to her and me and her and her client.

Long-term supervision

So I am very interested in 'the long haul' of being a supervisor for 35 years and also in having some long-term supervisees. In Chapter 7 one of Anna Chesner's supervisees refers to 'feeling very comfortable with Anna' having worked with her 'for a number of years' so was not only able to take her casework to supervision but also her feelings about leaving her current work and going freelance.

Focusing on this aspect of my work came as the result of a remark by Caroline, one of my long-term supervisees. Somehow the topic had turned to the notion that it was recommended to change one's supervisor about every three years. Caroline said she was glad that she hadn't known that as we would not have reached the level of relationship that we had now if she had had to change and that she did not believe it would have been possible to reach that level sooner. The relationship was related to the time we spent together which was then able to mirror and access the unconscious. It was as if the years needed to happen, for the earlier or more unconscious material to emerge. The same process, as she says, that happens with clients.

She writes:

> The importance of regular client supervision is unquestionable and forms a vital, nourishing, stimulating and supportive element of a therapist's practice. I can't imagine

working with long-term clients and not experiencing the same deep and meaningful process with my supervisor.

In fact, I question that I would be as well equipped to explore the unconscious alongside my clients, without having had this opportunity. Both my personal therapy and supervision inform me as psychotherapist. To my mind both require the same depth and intensity since the unconscious is always present and without long-term attention and 'presence', there are aspects of myself and my practice I would not have been able to access.

Undoubtedly there are arguments for changing supervisors, such as experiencing different styles of supervision and maybe accessing what John Rowan (1983) calls our 'deaf, blind and dumb spots' with a new supervisor. However, I find this argument less persuasive as my experience is that those blind, deaf and dumb spots travel on with us despite different supervisors and they are re-created in the instant of the first meeting. So far as I know there is not the equivalent belief that a client should change their therapist regularly; rather, it is more that they should not stay in therapy over-long. Maybe that is because therapy has grown out of a medical model or sickness model so health means not having therapy and having it means one is still sick or lacking. If we think in terms of relationships in our daily lives, we are usually looking for a long-term relationship with our husband or wife or children or parents. Certainly it is true with our relationship with ourselves, as we are stuck with ourselves whether we like it or not! So my belief is that it helps us if we have a relationship where that is modelled so we can explore it, comment on it and open our hearts to it. A relationship that we can stay with through 'thick and thin' rather than jumping out of it as soon as it does not work for us or feels uncomfortable. Of course this is very different from staying in a masochistic relationship. This premise I am looking at is explored by the Buddhist nun, Pema Chodrun (2001) and is illustrated by the title of her book, *The Wisdom of No Escape*. She says the way through to love is to have our heart broken open again and again until we can surrender to love.

I was sitting one evening at the end of a Playback training and it transpired that one of the group had been married for 28 years. When asked about it she commented that she had lived at least four marriages already! That's some of what I experience with my long-term supervisees and they with me. We have had several relationships already as I have had with them and with my own supervisors. In that sacred container I experience myself as non-judgmental almost all of the time, non-defensive, loving and loveable, open to what is rather than what should be; time slows down and the chance for exquisite attention both given and received happens almost all of the time. What more could I want? I experience regularly what Krishnamurti calls 'the highest form of human intelligence, the ability to observe without evaluating'.

Recently my co-supervisor was away for ten weeks. We usually meet every other Thursday for about two hours and have been doing now for nine years. At first I did not notice any difference in myself in my work as a therapist and supervisor. However, as the weeks went on I began to notice that sometimes I talked more in a session than I had intended, only a little, but it was there and then as the time went on I began to feel a little tired by the work and a little further on slightly 'burnt out', stressed and anxious, something I cannot say I have ever experienced before. Whatever ups and downs of mood and energy I feel in my own life this has almost never been the case with my work. At first I was puzzled and then it gradually trickled into my brain that I was not having regular supervision. And it wasn't the being stuck with clients or supervisees and needing to explore my countertransference or projections or needing help with generating other options or interventions. After many years of being a supervisor I have a well-developed internal supervisor who is good at that. No, it was the lack of holding, being seen and heard and being given loving, compassionate, ruthless attention by someone that had come to know me and my work over the years we had been meeting that I was missing; the turning up to the session, the other and myself and the mirroring, the attention and the unconditional regard.

I love the poetry of supervision and the cosmic moments of humour that my supervisees and I enter into, and I just love the rap. Judy Ryde, one of my co-tutors in the Centre for Supervision and Team Development, has what I think is a lovely definition of supervision. She sees it like Dr Who's Tardis, very small outside and timeless and huge inside. You come with an issue with your supervisee and there does not seem to be much room to move and as you step into it this huge space opens up inside. The way out is deeper in until, as the poet, Hafiz (1996), says we reach the point of:

> Pulling out the chair
> Beneath our minds
> And watching ourselves fall upon God –

> What else is there
> for 'Joan' to do
> That is any fun in this world!

References

Byron Katie (2002) *Loving What Is.* London: Rider.

Chodrun, P. (1991) *The Wisdom of No Escape.* London: Element.

Coltart, N. (1992) *Slouching Towards Bethlehem.* London: Free Association Books.

De Quincey, C. (2000) 'Exploring consciousness from the second person perspective.' *Journal of Transpersonal Psychology 32*, 2, 135–155.

Gilbert, M.C. and Evans, K. (2000) *Psychotherapy Supervision*, pp.3 and 82. Buckingham: Open University Press.

Hafiz (1996) *I Heard God Laughing*. Renderings of Hafiz by Daniel Ladinsky. Oakland, CA: Mobius Press.

Hellinger, B. (2006) *No Waves without the Ocean*. Netherlands: Kononklijke, Wohrmann, Zutphen.

Keats, J. (1819) *Ode to a Nightingale*.

Kohut, H. (1984) *How Does Analysis Cure?* Chicago, IL: University of Chicago Press.

Krishnamurti, J. 1895–1986. Quoted in Rosenberg, M. (2001) *Nonviolent Communication*, p.29. Del Mar, CA: PuddleDamer Press.

Lao Tzu 6th century BC.

Mason, B. (1993) 'Towards positions of safe uncertainty.' *Human Systems: Journal of Systemic Consultation and Management 4*, 189–200.

McTaggart, L. (2003) *The Field*. Wales: Cygnus Books.

Perls, L. Gestalt Therapist 1905–1990.

Rowan, J. (1983) *The Reality Game*, p.161. London: Routledge and Kegan Paul.

Rumi, J. 13th century.

Searles, H.F. (1975) 'The patient as therapist to the analyst.' In R. Langs (ed.) *Classics in Psychoanalytical Technique*. London: Hogarth Press.

The Harvard Negotiation Project: Stone, D., Patton, P. and Heen, S. (1999) *Difficult Conversations*. London: Penguin.

Yalom, J. (2001) *The Gift of Therapy*, pp.46, 68 and 72. London: Piatkus Books.

Further reading

Centre for Supervision and Team Development www.cstd.co.uk

Findhorn Foundation www.findhorn.org

Jones, J. and Wilmot, J. (2002) *The Boxing Clever Cookbook*. Scotland: J&J Publishing.

Playback Theatre (International Playback Theatre Network) www.playbacknet.org

Introduction to Chapter 6

Joe is the newest supervisor of the contributors and also focuses on the supervisory relationship. As a youth worker, Joe's style reflects his client group with a mixture of humour and directness. Because he is still in touch with starting to be a supervisor, he reminds us of some of the anxieties that a new supervisor might have. He describes how he works with them in a way that even experienced hands can learn from.

I asked Joe what he wanted the reader to get from reading his chapter and he replied:

> I want the reader to have fun. For me, writing this chapter was an enjoyable experience. I got to relive the excitement I felt starting out as a supervisor. Reflecting on what was important and what I had learnt along the way was very useful and also gave my passion a boost. I am still very new to supervision and indeed one lifetime may well not be long enough to become truly competent. One of the hardest tasks is coming to new clients, issues and experiences with the same freshness and enthusiasm one feels when something is new to us. I would like to think this chapter might act as a pleasurable reminder to the reader of what that experience can feel like.

Chapter 6

The Born Again Supervisor
Joe Wilmot

In this chapter I want to explore the experience of being new to supervision. As a fairly green supervisor I try to look at how I have developed in my practice and what I have found significant along the way. I begin by looking at my journey to becoming a supervisor and some of the problems I faced. An important aspect is focusing on the loving relationship which I see at the heart of good practice and indeed a good life. Towards the end I look at some of the lessons I have learnt and the beliefs and techniques which have developed from this learning.

The last thing I ever wanted to be was a supervisor. I had no interest in the caring professions and even less in people and their problems. As a child I saw humans as an undeserving species and focused my attention on the animal kingdom. My dream was to work in Africa saving the animals from the threat that people presented. Some of my mistrust and wariness was obviously due to my parents, as will become apparent later in this chapter. Indeed when I was about seven I saw the star chart my mother had done for me as a baby which stated that when I grew up my work would involve helping people. In disgust I vowed never to let the prophecy come true, so why am I writing a chapter about passionate supervision?

What can I say; things change. I am passionate about supervision and I am very passionate about supervision in my profession. I have been passionate ever since I received external supervision as a student when training to be a youth worker. This is a rare opportunity and one that is often only provided while studying. Now I supervise students, students with little or no experience of what supervision is or indeed what it can offer. They can be scared, confused and sometimes even resentful of having to be supervised at all (a state of mind which brings back childhood memories for me). My desire is for supervisees to experience what is possible within the supervisory framework, an experience that they cannot obtain in line management or performance reviews. There is usually a limit to how long I will see them for, so how do we move forward from the first guarded exchanges; what tools and techniques can help smooth the way and guide us through the supervisory encounter?

In the beginning

I am a youth worker in London and I work for my local council. All of my work is face-to-face with pupils who are at risk of being, or who have been, excluded from school. I find the work challenging, invigorating, despairing and deeply rewarding. The quality of youth work is very much linked to the abilities of those delivering. This does not mean that every youth worker has to be a natural, but rather that good practice must be shared and workers must be able to reflect and develop if they are to be of any use to the kids they work with. I was lucky that when I trained and qualified as a professional I was given external supervision as part of my course. I was also lucky to have a good supervisor who I liked and respected, which in turn contributed to supervision becoming an experience and a tool which I appreciated and valued highly. As I became a more accomplished youth worker and part of the management team for my borough I was given the chance to supervise youth workers who were in the process of qualifying at foundation level. I quickly jumped at the chance as I saw this as a real opportunity to develop my practice and gain some experience of being on the other side of the supervisory relationship. As the time approached I was suddenly struck by the realization that I was now, in part, responsible for the learning of these students and that I might be expected to say and know things that were meaningful, insightful and ultimately of consequence. This is something that preoccupied my cerebral capabilities while I waited for my first student to contact me and is indeed something which has preoccupied me ever since. In the meantime I was still waiting for a student to dazzle.

Delayed conception

In my fervour to execute my duties I had forgotten an important factor from my student days, which was that many of my fellow students had not been all that keen on supervision. They simply wanted to qualify as youth workers and did not understand how discussing their practice with someone unconnected with the course was going to help. What became apparent was that this was even more the case for some of the students on the foundation course. Due to new government targets many youth workers were being forced to qualify even if some of them didn't really want to. It appeared that my first supervisee might be one such worker. I waited, thought about what to do and waited some more. I spoke to other supervisors, some in the same position as me and realized that communication all round was fairly shaky in relation to the course. Some students and supervisors alike were unsure of arrangements; the course was a new one after all. In the end I called the student who seemed unaware of what was expected.

My first piece of supervision was to suggest she might contact the college that was running the course for clarity and then get in touch with me. Not exactly the tour de force with which I had intended to launch my new endeavour but at least the ball was rolling.

For the sake of the chapter I will call my first supervisee Mary. When we did finally meet I asked Mary what she knew about the purpose of these sessions. It quickly became clear that the college had not properly briefed her on the sessions or on supervision for that matter. My title was 'Personal Learning Facilitator (PLF)' and for Mary this meant she saw me as a personal tutor even though the outline for the role given by the college was very much in line with that of external supervision. My first task, as I saw it, was to talk a little about myself and my experience of supervision and what I thought the purpose of supervision was. At this moment I realized I was afraid. Here I was, a brand new supervisor who had only ever had one supervisor of his own, telling a youth worker with more years of experience than him what we should be doing in these sessions.

Family planning

It may not have escaped the reader that my surname is Wilmot and indeed Joan (one of the other authors) is my mother and Robin (another one) is my stepfather. Robin kindly asked me to write this chapter since I had collaborated on some other writing and he felt that I might offer a fresh perspective since many of the other authors had 'been around for rather a long time'. This seemed a little unfair on the others but I happily jumped at the chance. At one point he jokingly suggested I could include something along the lines of 'Born to Supervise'. I remember fixing him with one of my, apparently, less favourable looks as a more realistic title could have been 'Born to Run Screaming from Supervision'. As well as having supervisors/therapists for two of my parents, my father was a family therapist and my stepmother was a probation officer. From an early age I actively tried to avoid anything related to their work, although this was not always successful. I remember succumbing to Rebirth at four and Co-counselling at ten. After leaving home at 16 I embraced a varied array of activities, including managing a bar, and after a prolonged bout of travelling I found myself back in London employed by a local community centre at the age of 25.

Now this is not an academic book and if you want to look up the qualities needed to supervise you can find many good examples elsewhere. What I found important when I asked myself the question, 'Who am I to say what should happen in these sessions?' I was able to reflect in action (a favourite phrase on my course) and realize that I had relevant experience. I had studied supervision and been part of a good supervisory relationship. I did feel that I had a head start in terms of my upbringing and the relationships I had been part of. I also felt that my nature and the experiences I had gained in my life meant that I was open, observant, empathetic, patient (at times) and that I had something to contribute to the supervisory encounter. This was not merely an exercise in bolstering my confidence, but more a realization of my faith, not only in myself but in the supervisee and the process we were entering into. This was my first piece of real learning as a supervisor. I recognized that the supervisee and I would bring ourselves, our experience and our experiences; the key was to recognize, appreciate and work with this. By doing so my fear evaporated and we were free to explore the possibilities. It is interesting to note that this is a lesson I had learnt as a supervisee. Apparently I needed to learn it a second time from the position of supervisor.

Teething problems

Of course this was just the beginning of many challenges. After discussing supervision with Mary I asked her to tell me a little about her work and studies. It quickly became clear that she had quite a lot happening in her life. She was struggling to stay on the course, she was a single mother having problems with a teenage son and she was in the process of trying to change jobs due to difficulties with her manager. At this point I wanted to jump straight in and show Mary how extraordinary and useful the supervisory relationship could be, a chance to have a conversation that is honest, open and in the moment. I wanted her to experience the joy of having someone truly listening to her and what she had to say without stepping in and judging her actions. My next fear arrived: how were we going to do this? Now that we had discussed the purpose of supervision, we needed to agree on how we were going to practise it.

So how do you work together? What rules and guidelines are most likely to help you through this encounter? As I often find, inspiration comes from the kids and young people I work with. I and a colleague run personal development sessions in local schools with teenagers who are at risk of being excluded. The first session is always on boundaries. We have found it a good way to set the scene for all of the other sessions. By looking at boundaries we explore the beliefs and triggers of the young people we will work with, while giving them an impression of us and our work. At the end of the session we get everyone to write down boundaries and rules that the group will adhere to during the rest of our sessions.

Invariably the same rules, or variations of, always come up – allow people to have their say, respect others' opinions, encourage each other, confidentiality, come ready to participate. We very rarely have to prompt, as everyone has an idea of how they want to be treated and therefore how the group should behave. We then come together and agree on the ones we will use. The kids love it. They appreciate the fact that my colleague and I are working under the same rules as they are and this brings around an instantaneous change in them. By creating our own boundaries as a group, many of the rules and regulations they feel they have been labouring under suddenly evaporate. The framework of power has shifted for them and they become suddenly more open, approachable and indeed responsible. Nothing has actually changed apart from their frame of mind and they now feel capable and happy to police themselves; I have been caught out more than once (to their obvious amusement) when not abiding by the rules. It can be difficult not to fall into the role of expert sometimes when working with young people. You run the risk of telling them that what they have done or felt is right or wrong because you have more knowledge or experience. The part that I find interesting is that the rules agreed upon have common themes of trust, care and respect running through them, all the things you find in a healthy relationship.

I believe that loving relationships (with ourselves, each other and what we do) are the key to happiness. By being honest and open about who we are and what we need, life tends to be a lot more fruitful. I find that the supervisory relationship is no exception, and if anything demands this for any real level of satisfaction and/or success. It is important to work together to create a framework that you are both able to express yourselves, your ideas and your needs within. If punctuality is a problem for you (whether you demand it or find it hard to provide it) then this needs to be recognized and not left to become an issue. Lay your cards on the table but above all do it with love and care.

From speaking to other supervisors, and indeed supervisees, it is clear that some requirements within supervision sessions seem to be shared. Things like punctuality, booking and cancelling sessions can be seen as not much more than social etiquette but are often open to interpretation and can be a symptom of other issues. Mary was late two times out of the three and I can remember being annoyed and wondering how to tackle it. Why did I need to tackle it; mostly because I was annoyed about being annoyed which obviously wasn't helping. Often getting on and discussing it with love and care is the best and simplest option. Making a contract, formally or informally is something which is at the heart of the supervisory relationship and something that deserves attention.

I have often asked myself why I want or expect something from somebody. Anyone who has a friend they care about will know what it feels like to sometimes have different expectations and needs from them. This can often lead to difficulties if it is not dealt with in some way or other. As a supervisor I do believe you have an added responsibility to be aware of this dimension. To expect something simply because one does can be a dangerous assumption. Indeed convention, and the expectation that goes with it, can be one of the most crippling ailments to suffer from and one of the most damaging if the sufferer is a practitioner charged with the care or edification of others.

Early learning

Here are three examples that challenged my discernment of convention and the expectations I held in relation to my practice:

Example 1

Early on while working with Mary it became clear that her current post was causing a lot of problems for her and that most of them seemed to revolve around her manager. She said he was incompetent and that he was deliberately making her life difficult. It quickly became clear that regardless of her manager the real problem was how she managed herself. Another problem was that Mary knew I had worked with her manager before and that other colleagues had commented on how bad he was. Yet another problem was that she was quite right; in fact he was the worst manager and youth worker I had ever come across. Here is a section of a recording I made at the time of our second session:

> In relation to problems with line manager and previous job I still feel Mary wants me to reassure her of her actions. I tried to make it clear that whether I agreed or not was of no real consequence to supervision – i.e. how did it help her or her practice if I agreed? I did not know personally what had gone on and had no investment in what had happened.

I wanted to stay focused on Mary's practice and avoid judging situations I had not witnessed. After all I was there to supervise Mary and not her boss. When the third session started it was clear that Mary was more determined than ever to give examples of the manager's incompetence and so get me to have an opinion on the subject. I realized at that moment that I was being dishonest. Mary knew I knew the manager and therefore I had an opinion. This dynamic meant that if I avoided the subject then how could I expect Mary to be honest about her practice? I told her I thought he was a moron and should never have been given the job, and then I again asked her what difference this made to her and her practice. Only then did she realize that my opinion was of no use. The knock-on effect was that this helped her to see that many of her own opinions were not doing her much good either.

Example 2

A very interesting experience happened to me when I agreed to supervise someone who was also a friend. We weren't especially close but had known and liked each other for some time. Cas was an experienced youth worker and a Masters student studying Anthropology and Youth Work. She needed an external supervisor and asked me. Cas had not been through such a process and did not have much idea of how things might work. She first suggested we meet at a coffee shop to discuss things and I said maybe she should come to mine so that we could have some privacy. During our first encounter I explained how I thought the sessions should run, i.e. duration, format and process. Cas agreed but due to our being friends there was an informal element to our sessions. They were very relaxed; we drank coffee and at times discussed friends and other things outside of her practice. I did struggle with this but decided that it felt right for the circumstances. I was also not charging her as she had no money and I valued the experience.

It became clear that Cas could be very single-minded when helping her clients. She worked with young care leavers, and it often felt like she was crusading on their behalf. She stated on more than one occasion that she had come to blows with colleagues and managers because of the stance she took with some of her clients. During a session I asked Cas why she felt she had to save the young people she worked with. She struggled to explain why this was and the more I probed the further away I felt we were getting. I felt like we were on to something but was unsure of how to proceed. Right at this moment her mobile rang. In a normal supervision session this would have been embarrassing and maybe even a sign of unprofessional conduct. Cas happily went ahead and answered it; I did not feel comfortable in saying anything as I had allowed the relaxed style of our sessions to continue. What followed was one of the most bizarre phone conversations I had ever listened in on. It went something like this:

> Hello mum…I can't talk long…no I'm in a meeting…yes I've done it…no mum it's there…yes I've done that mum…did you call the doctor?…no I've done that mum…yes it's there, did you call the doctor?…mum, mum…yes mum I've done that…did you call the doctor?…

This went on and on; after a while Cas and I started laughing as things just seemed to be getting worse. It took Cas a good five minutes or more to placate her mother and get off the phone. Once we had finally stopped laughing and calmed down I asked Cas what the hell that was all about. Apparently her mother was very ill due to a severe drug habit that had been part of her life since before Cas was born. Her mother had been a heroin addict, but this had progressed through to an addiction to medication, and now her brain and organs were irreparably damaged. I asked her if she had always looked after her mother. Cas began to regale me with various stories of her mother and all the times she had looked after her and indeed saved her. It became clear that saving people was what Cas knew. This does not mean we should allow supervisees to behave however they like in the hope that this will result in enlightenment, but really it serves as a reminder that what we expect, require or demand can close us off to potential learning and development.

Example 3

Emma was a very capable youth worker and a conscientious student. She was also training to be a counsellor and had a superior grasp on what to expect from supervision. She diligently brought material from college and her work place for us to discuss and we both found the sessions productive and useful. However, during the fourth of six sessions, which took place over six months, she arrived in somewhat of a depressed and unfocused state. She attempted to discuss her practice but repeatedly struggled to gather her thoughts. She spoke negatively about her centre, her post, and the young people she was working with. She wasn't angry with anyone; rather she just seemed depressed by things in general. I knew that her job was causing her problems since her centre was being merged with another and the management team were not properly supporting her during this transition; however, we had discussed this in previous sessions and she had been objective and productive when tackling the various issues. I tried to help her with the problems she mentioned but after a while I realized that something else was going on. I decided to stop her and ask her what the real problem was.

Emma immediately apologized and said she was distracted because of losing her flat and was now struggling to find anywhere to live, plus she had to decide whether or not to move in with her boyfriend. I asked her if she wanted to talk about it. She said (with her knowledge of supervision and the difference between this and counselling) that she had worried it was not appropriate to bring this to supervision. I asked Emma if it was affecting her work. Of course it was; it was becoming increasingly difficult for her to work effectively with the young people and her colleagues due to the stress, and since she was not receiving proper managerial support it was just getting worse. I said it sounded like it was something that needed to be discussed for everyone's sake. We spent the rest of the session discussing her situation and looking at the options open to her, both in terms of her work and her personal life. Emma needed to be heard and our session provided an opportunity for that to happen. It can be difficult to know what is appropriate sometimes; as a youth worker I often find myself working in the 'grey areas'. All you can do is decide whether it feels right at the time and hope that you feel the same way afterwards. Trusting in yourself and the process is often the key to good work. Once again I believe this brings us back to the loving relationship. I did not know if discussing Emma's personal life was the right thing to do – all I knew was that it felt right; so I listened to Emma with love, care and attention.

Growing pains

So what should you discuss in supervision? Obviously your practice is the basis for everything, but what does that include? I remember the first time I went for supervision. I had started my youth work course and discussed with lecturers and fellow students what to expect. I also had my parents' experience to draw upon which meant that I had a good idea of what supervision was for and what sort of issues might arise. I arrived for my first session, met my supervisor, sat down and thought oh…what the hell happens now? It was at this moment that I realized that all the knowledge in the world makes no difference to the fact that you have to build a special kind of relationship with someone you have probably never met before in your life. We spent most of the hour simply trying to get to know one another. We did talk about the purpose of supervision and the role it had in my course, but the underlying feeling I took away with me was a sense of working out how we might communicate and whether I liked him. My first experience of supervising was indeed very similar.

Once I realized I liked my supervisor, my concern became that of bringing worthy material to our sessions. My supervisor was a busy manager in central London who ran a serious centre. He didn't want to listen to some trainee youth worker whingeing about cleaning toilets in his local community centre. I told myself I was an intelligent man who liked to ponder the big issues. I had a grasp of the current political climate and its effects upon youth work policy and delivery. We could have lively debates where we grappled with the existential fabric of our reality, leading to real insight and enlightenment for all…yeah sure we could. I remember a few sessions in, I had been struggling to find things to discuss since my course and my job were ticking along nicely, and I decided to launch into a monologue on the political and social pressures affecting the community centre I worked at. Various funding streams and having several organizations under one roof were leading to real difficulty in the running of the centre. I carried on for some time trying to demonstrate my understanding of the complex situation when my supervisor interjected. 'What has this got to do with young people? As a youth worker, how does anything you have been talking about benefit young people?' I was stumped. I had been talking about the centre I worked at, the staff, the politics, monetary constraints and everything else apart from how I was working with young people. It was a very grounding experience and one I try to remember at least once in a while. Supervision is about your practice. I am a youth worker, so what am I doing to fulfil that role?

My fear was around bringing things of genuine value to the sessions. The reality is that genuine value is to be found in the honesty and openness of the message. Language should be secondary to what you are saying. Sounding clever is nice at dinner parties, but even then most people listening will think you're a git. I think the fear of not being clever, or rather not being knowledgeable or skilled enough to supervise effectively, is at the heart of what concerns me when I allow fear to invade my thoughts. Certainly since I am fairly new to supervision I find that I question my ability; it is not so much about being up to the task but rather a fear that there is much I need to learn. This is a positive notion when I am thinking positively but left to my own devices I can create all manner of reasons why what I have said or done is inadequate or of little use. Reflection is a powerful tool which can be creative or destructive depending on your state of mind. Am I helping this person? Can I help this person? Why am I trying to help this person? Once again we are back to the 'grey areas'. I worry that I might be saying too much or too little; I worry that I'm telling stories because I like the sound of my own voice. I certainly worry about how much to share of myself since if I do share then who am I doing it for? Am I trying to impress them so that they think I am a fabulous and talented supervisor? At the end of the day it could all be true.

I like to think (when in positive mode) that I am gaining invaluable experience. Through experience and training I would hope to gain consistency and technique. For me, being and studying to be a youth worker gave my practice a depth and clarity which I do not feel could have happened otherwise. I try to embrace training opportunities when possible since this can only help to broaden my knowledge and experience but also because it helps to share the passion that people feel for their work. At the end of the day, though, conversations are the greatest resource I rely on. I make sure that there are established pathways for reflection and discussion. There are various people I seek out when in need; this can range from formal supervision through to a quick chat with the right person at the right time. The main component is the attention and awareness that this process requires for it to be productive. Sometimes a fleeting remark can be as, or more, revelatory than a serious brow bashing. So what has all this reflection done for me; what if anything have I learnt?

Loving relationships

While writing this chapter I sent an early unfinished draft to some of the other authors. Jochen kindly replied and sent me back the chapter with some comments. The main comment was around the fact that I supervise students on a short-term basis, sometimes only seeing them for six or eight sessions. He wrote, 'I would be very interested in this. How can I develop a relationship when there is hardly time to do so? Are there techniques to do that? Is there an advantage to having short-term supervision? Maybe in short-term supervision the relationship is not so important?' These are very useful questions and ones that I would like to try and answer.

The relationship is always at the heart of the supervisory encounter, but this does not mean that it is always the most important aspect. I believe that this is a significant factor to remember. When I am involved in short-term supervision with the students it has a defined purpose. I already know the duration of my time with them and I also have a clear idea of what I am trying to do. The supervisee is a student completing set modules. There are specific tasks and requirements that must be part of our sessions. I write statements on the students' progress which can be used as evidence in their portfolios. I am also responsible for evaluating their learning in relation to particular aspects of theory and practice. This structure provides guidance, objectives, boundaries and reassurance but it can also be limiting and indeed stifling. The clear structure provides a handy place to hide for the supervisee or indeed myself. If the student is to explore themselves in relation to their practice we must do more than tick the boxes.

On a practical level I take notes from my sessions so that I can use them to help me reflect; also I use them as a reminder when I next see the supervisee of where we were or might like to go. The reason I first started taking notes was that my supervisor had done so with me. When I started supervising I thought it might make me look more professional, like I knew what I was doing. It has since become a tool which I find very useful. Writing up your notes can also reveal more than you might think. I believe it is best to find your own way of writing things up, but when writing up sessions I use these four headings:

1. *Description* – describe what took place in the session.

2. *Feelings* – explore the feelings of the supervisee and yourself.

3. *Interventions and exploration* – what interventions were made, explore incidents/aspects of the session that you felt were important.

4. *Conclusions/further action* – try to bring things together and look for learning and development.

This can be a laborious task and may seem rather like the box ticking I mentioned. I don't always write up sessions, but when I do I often discover I have learnt something that I would have otherwise missed. I find that freedom can often be found in structure and this is what I meant when I spoke of the freedom of short-term supervision. I don't have to worry about whether we get on that much. I know there will be things to discuss and that I have a defined purpose as a 'Personal Learning Facilitator'. If it seems right to focus on the nuts and bolts then so be it, or we can leave the path and explore. The relationship can be important or not depending on the supervisee and what we focus on in the session. Some students have never really looked at themselves; some can't stop. Paradoxically, one aspect of short-term supervision which can often be freeing is the lack of time itself. Necessity being the mother of invention means that as a supervisor I found myself compelled to act upon my instincts. Earlier in the chapter I wrote 'Lay your cards on the table but above all do it with love and care'. This is most certainly the case when you only have a few sessions in which to do so. There isn't necessarily time to let things develop naturally. I must quickly make clear to the supervisee what my understanding is of what we might try and achieve, but also that they have a responsibility to do the same. In the case of Emma, if there had been more time I might have not said anything when she seemed distracted in our fourth session and the opportunity would have been lost. If I had no idea of how long I might see a supervisee I could well spend more time worrying about what they thought of me and whether I was doing any good.

So, what is good about the supervision I find myself practising? The last note I made for this chapter was 'maintaining the passion in such a quick formal experience of supervision', but of course I am not maintaining the passion in these quick and formal sessions at all. The students I supervise are often far from passionate about coming to see me. Just as I first became passionate about supervision as a student, I realize that the real challenge is trying to ignite the passion in the supervisee. By doing this I also fuel and maintain my own passion which, for me, completes the cycle. This is at the heart of my passion; it is the perpetual exchange of knowledge and experience which brings out the best in people and practice. Wow, I sound like a tree hugger (oh God, I'm turning into my parents).

Introduction to Chapter 7

Anna moves us on to using techniques from the creative therapies in supervision; psychodrama in particular. I first met her as a trainer of Playback Theatre, a form of improvisation theatre that elicits stories from the audience and plays them back in a way that is cathartic and healing. She is passionate about using action methods where appropriate and the value of showing and creating, as well as talking. She explains the philosophical underpinning of her work, and in her detailed vignettes she adds the supervisees' accounts to her own, which contributes another important dimension.

I asked Anna what she most wanted the reader to gain from reading her chapter and she answered:

> ...that creativity and spontaneity belong in the supervisory relationship and that the judicious use of psychodramatic action methods opens new perspectives for supervisee and supervisor.

Chapter 7

Psychodrama: A Passion for Action and Non-action in Supervision

Anna Chesner

I write here about the philosophical underpinning of my approach to supervision, based in the core values of creativity and spontaneity; in particular the choice to use or refrain from using a variety of action methods. I give examples of my learning from the role of supervisee as well as from my supervision practice with groups and individuals. I have included supervisees' own accounts of their experience using psychodramatic action methods in their sessions with me, which facilitated a change of perspective and clarification of role.

I have been supervising for nearly 20 years, and I am still passionate about it. What maintains my passion is when I witness myself making a difference; especially when my response to a supervisee or supervision group provokes my *creativity* and *spontaneity* to offer a new form or intervention, supported by my understanding and experience of role theory and psychodramatic technique. At moments like this we are discovering together. These sessions are energizing and tend to be remembered for longer than 'routine' sessions, although the routine sessions provide the underpinning to the more memorable ones.

At the heart of my personal value system is my passion for creativity and spontaneity in my work and life, whether in the field of psychotherapy, supervision, consultation or performance. Psychodrama as a core philosophy and practice emphasizes these two values. Indeed psychodrama has been described as 'The Passionate Technique' (Williams 1989) so the idea of passionate supervision fits well with my core values.

My beliefs about good practice

Let us look at the definition of spontaneity in the words of the founder of psychodrama: '[Spontaneity] propels the individual towards an adequate response to a new situation or a new response to an old situation' (Moreno 1953, p.42).

True spontaneity means being appropriate to the moment, meeting the moment with openness and energy that is 'fit for purpose'. This means that the use of psychodramatic or action methods in supervision is not a habit but a choice; like a much loved condiment added to a meal, it loses its impact if applied willy-nilly, but can bring out the other flavours present if chosen with care. I find that practitioners who work a lot in action benefit from a space to reflect verbally on their practice, so abstinence from the very methods I am passionate about can in itself be a passionate choice.

How supervision has held me

One of the perspectives from which I evaluate and reflect on my own approach to supervision is from my experience in the counter-role, that of supervisee. I have benefited from supervisors meeting me from a perspective I was not expecting – addressing a blind spot in effect. None of the following examples that I recollect from my life as a supervisee are rocket science, yet they were of considerable value to me. They are each an example of the supervisor being in-tune in the relationship with me, while sufficiently distanced to offer a new perspective, and in two cases practical advice.

The first example was when I was setting up practice again after a period living and practising abroad. Having experienced the loss of a relationship, a home and a network of practice, my personal focus was on surviving the transition – setting up practice in London, getting on with it at a practical level. My supervisor gently but firmly recommended I consider returning to therapy or analysis, and even made a recommendation as to who might be suitable. I followed this up, and benefited both personally and professionally from this nudge.

Another example of supervision offering a new perspective was when being supervised by someone working primarily in organizational development. She was attuned to the organizational aspects of my practice and got me to use pen and a large sheet of paper to look at the realities of my practice in terms of time commitment, financial remuneration and other rewards. This helped me realize that I had the freedom to make choices that suited me, supported me, and the development of my practice in a desired direction. I do not now remember the precise changes I made, but I internalized the sense of permission and personal responsibility, and there have been many times since when I have taken stock of the shape of my practice as a whole and made in-principle decisions to change priorities. This supervisor helped me develop the role of 'conscious and responsive shaper of my practice'. We all have over-developed, under-developed and adequate roles. Supervision has the function of giving a perspective on these as applied to our professional and clinical practice.

A third example of a moment in my life as a supervisee, which sparked a moment of insight, involved a simple affirmation of my skill in a particular intervention. I have the tendency in my psychotherapy practice to gloss over what I do well in a moment of inspiration, and to focus on where my challenges are. In this instance I was presenting a first post-assessment session with a client who was clearly very anxious. This manifested in a tide of self-interrupting talk that made communication difficult. In psychodramatic terms I would say he had an 'over-developed verbalizing self-analyser role'. The anxiety in the room was palpable and the client began the session with a lengthy self-questioning speech, verging on the paranoid. At this early stage in the therapy I wanted to take some basic historical details in a genogram, and so asked him to choose an object in the room (my consulting room is furnished with hundreds of small models and props suitable for use in symbolic representation) to concretize his anxiety and to give it a place. He chose a model of a bird and gave it a place on a shelf, where it could view proceedings, but was in effect separate from him, thus enabling us to engage in a two-way conversation. I mentioned this intervention in passing in my supervision, and found myself feeling dismissive of my supervisor's genuine praise for the intervention. When it was later mentioned for a second time I allowed myself to take it in and to feel supported by my own strengths in my practice. On reflection I realize that this shift in my own ability to acknowledge what I was doing well mirrors the client's process of creating some perspective on his anxiety and allowing himself the space to contact more functional and supportive roles.

Vignettes from the role of supervisor

I will now describe three vignettes of working with psychodramatic action methods, which felt different and made a difference.

The first example comes from a group supervision setting within an academic environment. Participants were intermediate level counselling trainees, some with considerably more clinical experience than others. The training organization had developed an interesting reflective tool for case presentations, in which trainees presented background to a client, and verbatim extracts from the session. The group would then reflect together about the presentation with the trainee following the discipline of 'just listening' and then reporting back considered reflections the following week. On a number of occasions I have found it invaluable to break the form of this habitual way of working (what Moreno would call a 'cultural conserve'[1] and direct a psychodramatic exploration of the material.

Vignette 1: Reflection through action methods

A trainee had expressed an interest in beginning to learn to work with dreams. The presentation she had made featured

---

1 The whole notion of cultural conserve is relevant to supervision. It relates to structures and forms that originate in spontaneity and creativity, but which become habitual and so lose their appropriateness to the moment. Moreno writes 'The cultural conserve renders to the individual a service similar to that which it renders as a historical category to culture at large – continuity of heritage – securing for him the preservation and the continuity of his ego. This provision is of aid as long as the individual lives in a comparatively still world: but what is he to do when the world around him is in revolutionary change and when the quality of change is becoming more and more a permanent characteristic of the world in which he participates?' (Moreno 1940 in Fox 1987, p.46). Surely this is a key function of supervision, to release the stickiness of our cultural conserves in clinical practice and create space for the flow of creative thought and action.

a client whose dreams were full of water, and whose symptomatology also included a particular relationship with the bathroom. The intervention I suggested to explore the client world and the therapeutic relationship more deeply as a group involved isolating a number of metaphors and images from the client's dream life, family constellation, and narratives of her current issues. Each of these was embodied by one or two group members – producing an array of potent physical sculpts, enhanced by a word or sound suggested by the supervisee or one of the trainees in role. The supervisee was invited to witness the range of these images, to walk around the space and view them from different perspectives, and to engage in dialogue with any parts of the whole constellation that intrigued her. In a couple of instances I invited her to role reverse, i.e. physically to enter the world of the client through the image and find some answers to her own questions in this way. These role reversals were brief, as I did not think it would be helpful to enter the client's disturbance so deeply that the supervisee might lose perspective on her own role, or indeed trigger personal material inappropriate to the supervision setting and relationship.

The feedback from the supervisee and group after this intervention was enthusiastically positive. They felt energized by the action approach, and experienced a more deeply felt connection with the material presented. The session remained a point of reference for the group after the event. The process of physicalizing an image helps keep it 'in mind'. The intervention as a whole promotes 'action insight', a concept rooted in the psychodramatic method, and defined by Kellerman as 'the integration of emotional, cognitive, imaginary, behavioural and interpersonal learning experiences.' (Kellerman 1992, p.86).

For me, sensing the *appropriate* timing and intensity of action-based interventions, and fine-tuning them to the needs of the specific context, is satisfying in terms of my own practice. It is a question of aesthetics, of finding an appropriate form for that moment. The structure of the intervention is spontaneous and its application in the moment is a function of many years' practice with these methods in the context of psychotherapy, supervision and performance. I enjoy the multi-layered awareness of such moments, in which I am evaluating (a) the spontaneity levels of a group new to these methods, and relatively new to counselling; (b) the capacity of the supervisee, whose client work is being explored, to deal with a more intense encounter with the material being presented. At the same time, I experience myself as being both a part of the group as a whole (one facet of a multi-faceted reflecting crystal), and to be the holder of a particular meta-perspective, what Couroucli-Robertson calls the 'helicopter ability' (Couroucli-Robertson 1999). The whole group witnesses and reflects on the unfolding representation of the inner and outer worlds of the client and client/counsellor system. In this sense the group itself partly performs the function of supervisor; at the same time my responsibility in role as group supervisor is to 'mind the shop' in a more active way; to make sure we maintain the boundaries of the session in terms of time and focus, and manageability for the participants. I believe that this role is especially important when using methods that are experiential and in some ways freer or more open than the traditional talking approach.

When I reflect on my passion and enthusiasm for such an approach I recognize that it is paralleled by what stretches and excites me about my psychotherapy practice, where I often find myself with a foot in two worlds – the abstract world of words and the concretized world of symbols; the world of the individual and that of the group; the relationship between protagonist and myself as psychodrama director and the relationship between protagonist and group as witnesses and co-creators.

REFLECTIONS ON KEY MOMENTS CHOSEN BY SUPERVISEES

I have invited two supervisees to share their reflections on key sessions or interventions in their supervision with me. Their response was enthusiastic and generous, which in itself is a reminder of the importance and benefit of reviewing the supervision process from time to time, particularly with long-standing supervisees. I was excited to do this as I was curious to see whether we had the same ideas as to what constituted key moments in the work, and whether our perspectives on what happened were similar. Their words are included, in edited version, as quotes.

Vignette 2: A matter of perspective

I am passionate about the possibility of creating a shared visual and symbolic language through the use of small objects in supervision, to communicate and discover. This is an example of a satisfying session in which the method chosen facilitated an important insight into the matter of perspective.

Helen is a team leader in charge of a number of professionals, trainees and volunteers delivering therapeutic services in a school setting. As such she is employed by an external agency to set up this provision from scratch and create a difference within the school culture. By profession she is an art therapist and, while she has experience as a clinician, this is her first job in a combined clinical and managerial role. She had been bringing both clinical and team issues to supervision and on this occasion began the session by recognizing that after a period of feeling very stressed and overwhelmed by the challenges of the work she was beginning to recognize the magnitude of what she had taken on and what was being asked of her. She asked to spend the session exploring this.

What emerged felt satisfying to both of us: an example of creative flow leading to a potent visual image, and this facilitating reflection and insight.

For me, the choice of form is a creative challenge. I gave myself a moment to reflect on what method might best suit her purpose. This supervisee was immersed in a context and a setting, which was new to her and complex. When choosing an action-based method, I bear in mind the question of aesthetic distance; would she benefit from raising her empathy levels and getting closer to or inside the clients' or colleagues' perceptual world; or would it be better to help her gain a more distanced perspective? What was clear to me was that she needed to locate herself in relation to the system as a whole, so that she could engage with it from a place of personal centredness.

These considerations led me to suggest she explore her question through the 'communicube'. This is a transparent cube shaped structure consisting of five 'floors' or levels spaced a few centimetres above each other forming a small coffee table sized cube. Its distinctive feature is that it allows the user to create five separate spectograms or miniature sculpts, one above the other, and that the transparency of the plastic material allows the interrelationship of the five images to be visible. It is a tool developed by my colleague John Casson, which I have found useful from time to time when looking with supervisees or therapy clients at complex multi-layered systems or perspectives.

I invited Helen to keep in mind the focus of the session, i.e. 'What have I taken on in this job?'

I left it to her to decide how she would use each layer of the communicube, trusting that the pertinent issues would become apparent to both of us in the unfolding. In summary: she began at the top level with a depiction of the 'heavy brigade', the top management system at the school and within Helen's agency, peopled by gladiators and rhinos. It was an image of a political dynamic, which Helen did not understand but intimated.

Level two, just below, was filled with stones, little animals, human and gnome-like figures. I watched as Helen kept adding more and more. I even wondered whether she had forgotten that there were three more levels to use. Eventually she explained to me that this level represented the children and their therapeutic needs, and so by extension the families with their psychosocial situations, violence, abuse, language difficulties, housing difficulties; also the teachers with their personal and professional concerns and the therapeutic team. It was an extraordinary image of clutter and complexity – all human life was here!

I asked Helen where she was in this, and she answered the question by working on the third and central level of the sculpt. This level represented her managerial and clinical roles. There was noticeably more space and aesthetic design to this level, a sense of breathing space. She chose two miniature canvas bags with tiny worry dolls in them, to represent herself and her closest colleague, and some carefully chosen small crystals and glass pieces to represent her team and their case load.

At this point from my position as reflective witness, it seemed to me that Helen had a spontaneous and important thought. She turned to me and said with some emotion that she had not done any of her own art since she had started the job. Her own creativity expressed through art is important to her not only as a resource for her clinical role but for its own sake and for her personal development. She represented this on the fourth level down with a packet of seeds, an artificial leaf and a conker from my props, and reaching into her own bag a large golden autumn leaf. I recalled her words at the start of the session that she had been 'playing' in the park just before the session, that autumn leaves still filled her with delight. The spirit of creative play is indeed a vital resource and something that I passionately resonate with.

The first four levels were complete and we began to reflect on them. Helen was sitting on the floor from where she had a good view into each level. She identified the middle level as the heart of her task at the school, that she is a clinician and team leader first and foremost. By concretizing the other perspectives she was formulating her own priorities. She was able to see the dangers of getting over-identified or concerned with the perspective from top management, and to recognize the value of seeing the *details* of the system (at level two). Although the details could feel overwhelming, she had been able to identify therapeutic need among children whose need might not have been noticed by other colleagues in the system, children who were withdrawn and quiet rather than those exhibiting challenging behaviours. She asserted her priority to be the clinical work (at level three) supported by her own creativity (at level four). She completed the sculpt by laying some beads and a tangle of tape at the bottom level of the cube to represent the underlying feeling of the impact of the work, and perhaps as a reminder to beware of becoming entangled.

I wondered what it was that made this supervision session satisfying. Helen said that the visual image would stay with her and that if she found herself in a similarly complex setting or in similar dynamics at some future stage of her career she would recognize it more quickly. It would act as a marker for her. In retrospect she summarized the significance:

How can I, my team, this project survive when we are so small in among the hierarchy of the school, among the deprivation, neglect, abuse and mental health issues that appear to dominate the children, staff and families?... In fact here it stands, our project, centralized. The larger figures are not trampling on the smaller ones; they are perhaps holding something even bigger than us. I am not only surviving, I am an entire level in the cube beneath my work...the leaf I have brought in from the park symbolizes something external to the cube, for I am not alone. I have my family, my co-workers, my therapy, and my supervision. All form separate cubes of their own. In fact the cubes could begin to stack as survival spans out into an entire system, in which I, my team and our project are very much alive.

For me the session was satisfying for three reasons. First, I felt I had offered the supervisee an appropriate structure for exploring her theme, and my trust in the structure was rewarded. Second, there was a sense of the implicitly known taking form before our eyes and becoming more explicitly known and understood, i.e. this was a creative event. Third, it was holistic. I am passionate about the importance of the practitioner's own creativity and life values having a place in their work. So, when Helen recognized the importance of doing her own art and when her pre-session moment of play came into the session in the form of her autumn leaf, this affirmed something quite central to me personally and philosophically.

In terms of action – the moment of greatest activity for me was in choosing the form. During the creation of the sculpt my role was to witness, hold the space and ultimately co-reflect with the supervisee. In subsequent sessions we have referred to the image of the five level sculpt, which has helped us locate our focus within a sense of the system as a whole. This has been particularly important when the temptation has come up to get over-involved in the political levels of the setting. In this way the work of the one session underpins and remains present in the continuing work.

Vignette 3: A personal/professional crisis

This vignette demonstrates the delicate balancing act that occurs when a supervisee brings an issue on the boundary of therapy and supervision. There are always choices to be made about focus and form. In this session I made a choice to invite three different degrees of aesthetic distance to the personal material in the light of the supervisory setting.

RUTH'S INTRODUCTION

This was my first session with Anna, since I had been retired. Retirement was not of my choice; the agency I worked for was in grave financial difficulties but also I was the deputy director to someone I had lost respect for, and no longer felt that she was trustworthy or possessed integrity. I had actually wanted to go part-time, but partly because the agency was in such a mess I had not voiced this. It had been a considerable shock on return from holidays to hear that I was to be retired on my birthday, which was less than three months away. I was very concerned about leaving my team, who I knew would be very fearful of the future. However, this was not my only concern; I had been an employed person for 28 years, and while I was happy not to work full-time, I felt quite concerned about launching into consultancy and private work after all that time. Also I was feeling deskilled, not valued; my self-esteem seemed to have plummeted. This was a new feeling for me as I normally was pretty confident about my skills and abilities. These feelings I kept to myself. While I was happy to talk about going on a superficial level, the more negative feelings I shared with no-one. Why? Perhaps I felt ashamed of them; I did not even voice them to my partner.

RUTH'S FEELINGS

For the first time in my experience of Ruth, whom I have known for a number of years as a supervisee and as a supervision trainee, Ruth was tearful. Ruth describes herself as 'not particularly emotional' and her clear distress at the start of this session helped me make the decision to offer her an intervention to do some personal work on her changing professional identity at this time. Ruth has in the past brought material to supervision that is highly emotive in content. She has for many years worked with children whose family and social situations are almost unbearable to think about, whose behaviour is often disturbed; yet who in their play therapy with her make the most vivid and touching stories and pictures, through which they express their distress and their move towards healing and integration. In presenting this work she comes across as contained, thoughtful, empathic and very boundaried. We have often shared verbally how moved or appalled we are at someone's life situation, but I had never before seen her in her own distress.

My thinking was that we would be able to unpack what was distressing Ruth at a feeling level and then hopefully reflect on the underlying issues together. I asked her to represent her feelings about herself in the first instance. She took a black waste paper bin, covered it in a black cloth and placed a mask on top of it looking inward. This use of symbolization helped her show then verbalize her sense of mourning for what she had lost and her feeling of being 'useless' and 'finished'. She saw herself as something rubbished and finished with. 'To be retired' was to be rejected and dumped. This blow had put her in touch with her own wounded child role in a most powerful way. I felt that acknowledging and literally giving space to the feelings allowed us then to consider the rest of the system for Ruth.

Other elements Ruth symbolized in the space were the children and families she works with, the agency director with whom there was a mutually felt and unspoken coolness; and the issue of having to charge money for her work once she started to work in private practice.

The question of aesthetic distance was a useful guide for me in facilitating Ruth through the work. The initially overwhelming feelings were put 'out there' – potent but at one remove. I believe that the physical and aesthetic activity of choosing and laying out symbols for this reflective work begins to shift the physical and emotional energy and mental state of the supervisee. In terms of role we can see this as a shift from the 'overwhelmed and rejected child' to the 'creative expresser and reflector'.

The clients and appreciative colleagues presented a different kind of opportunity in terms of aesthetic distance, a choice for minimal distance. By encouraging her to speak in role reversal as the clients and colleagues she had worked with I was able to invite her to challenge her view of herself as being on the scrapheap. Her first access to a more realistic and positive self-view was, interestingly, through the eyes of others, clients and colleagues who know her value.

We unpacked the issue of Ruth's parental conditioning around money and being 'in business' through discussion rather than role reversal; a choice for greater aesthetic distance I made in the light of this being a supervision session rather than a therapy session. While role reversing with parental figures could have taken us into therapeutically interesting early material, I felt that discussion and direct challenge suited the supervisory setting better. As somebody in private practice myself, whom Ruth respects, I used my own experience to talk about the issues of invoicing, handling money and self-valuing in professional practice, in order to engage her in re-considering her prejudice against therapist/consultant as business person.

RUTH'S REFLECTION ON THE VALUE OF THE WORK

It was quite amazing how free I felt after the session; it was as if a lightness had entered me, removing the heavy burden that had been present. I felt energized, no longer trapped and useless. I was able to acknowledge the skills and knowledge that I had, the money issue was no longer an issue, and yes of course I would charge the appropriate rate. I also felt myself virtually straighten up; I felt me again.

It is now almost two months since I left the agency. I am in the process of building up work. Colleagues from social services and from the universities, when they heard I was leaving have been keen to enlist me for work, and I am building up contacts and work, which enables me to work two to three days a week.

I created my own business cards, which I delight in spreading around, and am in the process of devising my own invoices so as to bill my clients.

What emerged in this session was the transformation of perspective. Something that was experienced as a death changed into a kind of birth. As Jochen Encke remarked in an authors' meeting, 'In this session the egg-shell broke'.

Conclusion

In writing about what I am passionate about in supervision, I have characteristically chosen to look at work in action, with several contrasting examples of what I do and why I think I do it. This reflects my belief that 'showing' or 'creating' often brings more information into the frame than 'talking'. The work with Ruth and Helen demonstrates a choice for action in the session as a creative resource to facilitate a shift in their understanding and feeling states. Action in their cases took the form of working with the communicube, sculpting, concretizing and role reversal.

Since creative action approaches bring an extra dimension to the process of supervision, appreciated by both supervisor and supervisee, why do I not use these approaches all the time? Sometimes the priority for the supervisee is simply to offload or download: to have their work witnessed in some way rather than necessarily to explore an issue in depth.

I have noticed this particularly with some supervisees who work in isolation rather than as a member of a team. At other times there is no clear question or focus and the value is in reflecting together in a free-floating way. This process may lead to a focus for creative intervention in a future session. Some practitioners work so much in action and enactment that the opportunity to talk about the work provides the balance needed; an opportunity to tease out the layers of the work in discussion together, to reflect in terms of theoretical understanding and practical techniques: to think and talk rather than to act. If I were to insist on always finding an action-based supervision form for these sessions this would be to make the choice for action methods a cultural conserve. My hope rather is to manifest my commitment to the psychodramatic philosophy of spontaneity and creativity in my work as a supervisor: to attempt to find the appropriate and adequate response to each new supervision situation.

Acknowledgements

Thanks to Helen Cross, Beverley Rees, and Ruth Watson, who generously shared their reflections with me.

References

Couroucli-Robertson, K. (1999) 'Supervisory triangles and the helicopter ability.' In E. Tselikas-Portmann (ed.) *Supervision and Dramatherapy.* London: Jessica Kingsley Publishers.

Kellerman, P. (1992) *Focus on Psychodrama: The Therapeutic Aspects of Psychodrama.* London: Jessica Kingsley Publishers.

Moreno, J.L. (1953) *Who Shall Survive? Foundations of Sociometry, Group Psychotherapy and Sociodrama.* New York: Beacon.

Moreno, J.L. (1940) 'Spontaneity and catharsis.' In J. Fox (ed.) (1987) *The Essential Moreno.* New York: Springer.

Williams, A. (1989) *The Passionate Technique.* London: Routledge.

Introduction to Chapter 8

Lia, in her words, sees passion for change as synonymous with passion for life as process. She describes helping supervisees change by assisting them in questioning their belief systems and checking tacit systems, expectations and points of interest. She brings into her chapter her experiences of Gestalt, phenomenology, new physics, poetry and drama.

When I asked Lia what she most wanted the reader to gain from reading her chapter, she answered:

> I would like the reader to appreciate how I see supervision as a creative, challenging and enthralling process of discovery in relationship.

Chapter 8

The Passion for Change:
A Life Story
Lia Zografou

I am writing about my passionate regard for change in my supervision practice. I relate aspects of my personal journey trying to comprehend the intricacies of change as a process of life in general and the supervisory relationship in particular. I would like the reader to follow my course of expanding my understanding of change as I explain how modern physics, Gestalt therapy, phenomenology, dramatherapy and theatre practice have influenced my role as supervisor. I mainly explore change as a process of awareness in the moment and give examples of how dramatic structures, playful engagement and attending to the physical aspect of communication can further the supervisee's and supervisor's awareness and release blocks to creative intervention.

I am passionate about change. Change fascinates me not only as an existential issue, the backbone of my lived experience in the world, but also as the central premise, cause and process of my professional life.

My desire to train in therapy and supervision dates back to my adolescent preoccupation with fundamental existential questions. How do I know who I am? How do I know the world? How do I relate to the ever changing landscape of people, situations, conflicts and emotions that surrounds me? What changes in me and how? I recall how my passion for such questions began when I first read T.S. Eliot's poetry. I was deeply moved by his call to continue the exploration in order to return to 'where we started and know the place for the first time' (Eliot 1944, *Little Gidding*). The paradoxical ending of this verse caused a powerful stir in me. I remember thinking, as a 15-year-old, 'Is it possible to think and feel about my present situation in a totally different way? If so, how? I can't for the life of me imagine a different way of seeing my present'. How is this freshness of eye and mind that Eliot encourages to be captured, nurtured, evoked?

It was around that time that I discovered the language of theatre. My adolescent involvement with drama became a passion which I pursued professionally for a number of years before I discovered yet another, even more compelling and fulfilling platform of expression in dramatherapy. My studies of both drama and dramatherapy advanced my perception of change as something fluid and multifarious which could be well served by dramatic action. More and more I recognized that what we conceive as 'real' and 'true' may be represented in various ways, all equally valid in their interpretations and each carrying an aspect of reality. A piece of theatre, with its multiplicity of voices and points of view, offers access to linguistic and symbolic representations of a plethora of 'truths' that pertain to any particular phenomenon.

Working with drama in my capacity as actor, director and dramatherapist I was humbled by theatre's ingenious ability to contain the fluidity and complexity of human experience. While working with the same theatrical piece, I embodied a different truth as actor, a very different one as audience and an even more varied and complex reality as dramatherapist. As a dramatherapist I developed the skill of being an empathic theatre director, someone who will offer her clients various possible means to discover the apposite metaphors, symbols and dramatic forms which will meaningfully represent their experiences until they reach new insight, new knowledge and new stability. Dramatherapy taught me to be resourceful, patient and suspend interpretation. I learned to trust that deep engagement with our creativity will transform and enrich our experience.

As I observed my clients' struggles to represent their emotional and physical reality through the language of metaphors I realized that change, this elusive, often chaotic concept, could be addressed very simply through awareness of 'what is happening right now'. I watched my clients sigh with tremendous relief when an internal knot was finally untied, as they discovered their own meaningful way to symbolize their troubled situation. I began to investigate my role in their change of perceptions. How was I being helpful? How was I facilitating awareness? This shift in my thinking was further facilitated by my interest in science and theoretical physics in particular. Reading about chaos theory and cybernetics along with quantum physics, I came to appreciate the new paradigm in thought which views life as a self-organizing system of interconnected parts, ever-changing and ever-relating. I thus gave up on any grandiose expectations of ever fixing my perception of the 'real' because, as Heisenberg's uncertainty principle shows, by observing something I have already changed it through my relationship to it (Capra 1996).

But most importantly (and with considerable resistance), I gave up on my old idea that change is something I can willfully engineer. I now understand change as a process which occurs irrespective of my actions. My mere existence is sufficient cause for altering the dynamics of any situation, however small or imperceptible. The great challenge is to remain aware and perceptually alert to recognize and incorporate the small changes which occur around me all the time. This is what I perceive as the challenge of relating consciously. My focus is on locating my position in relation to the other and clarifying the rules that define our relationship. I pride myself in thinking that I am gradually approaching what Eliot called finding 'the still point in a turning world' (Eliot 1944, *Burnt Norton*). In practice I discovered that my role in facilitating change in my clients rested more with the quality of my presence rather than any ingenuity in intervention. When I was alert, curious, engaged and open both mentally and physically, my clients responded with less anxiety, more spontaneity and considerably more willingness to experiment and explore alternative possibilities, thus entering the world of 'as if', the potential space of playfulness, creativity and competency (Winnicott 1971).

In conjunction with dramatherapy and modern science, my studies of Gestalt therapy and phenomenology supported my understanding of change even more. Gestalt therapy, in the paradigm of modern ecology, regards humans as unique self-organizing and self-regulating systems capable of choosing a life course for themselves according to their needs and perceptual idiosyncrasies in time. The term 'Gestalt' is a German word which refers to a clear, emerging perceptual form or figure. This figure may be an external object, such as a shape, or an internal one, such as one's childhood, emotional state, desire or need. The goal of Gestalt therapy is to assist people in forming clearer figures for themselves and by doing so, to help them make better, responsible choices about the way they contact the environment and attend to their needs (Perls, Hefferline and Goodman 1951). Fritz Perls, the creator of Gestalt therapy, claimed that the best intervention from the therapist (or parent, or supervisor) was asking three simple questions, at the appropriate times:

1. What are you aware of 'right now'?

2. What do you want 'right now'?

3. How are you stopping yourself from getting it 'right now'? (Perls 1973).

The questions draw attention to the emerging figure in time and facilitate its full articulation in language. The need is allowed to emerge without criticism. The clearer the need, the clearer we can see it for what it is and the easier we can relate to it. Once we have a clear figure in mind, we have already begun to change, first by changing our perception of it and then by changing our relationship to it. A paradoxical phenomenon is at hand: change occurs without deliberately contriving it. Gestalt theory suggests that the route towards meaningful change is through awareness of how things are in the present and not through attempting to turn them into how we'd like them to be in the future.

The influences I presented above have been the maps I have been following as a supervisor confronted with the dynamics of change on a regular basis. 'How do I cope with this...', 'how may I facilitate that...', 'what does my client need when she behaves like this...', are some of the more frequent questions which enter the supervisory relationship. Inherent in all these concerns is a difficulty on the part of the supervisee to contemplate, address or manage a situation that requires a change in perceptions of self, other or the present reality.

I could assume a didactic role and offer a long list of possible solutions, educative answers or pearls of wisdom from my own professional experience. None, however, would serve my supervisee's need for deeper understanding and meaningful change in his/her perceptions and strategies. Also, I feel that the session would be dull and stale, without any prospects of surprise or fascinating discoveries for either of us and, quite plausibly by extension, the client as well. I receive the challenge with relish and opt for a more explorative route. I remain as impassionate an observer as I can and dwell on the problems presented from a position of total ignorance. 'I don't know. Let's look at what is here' is my first intervention. At this moment I am as open as I can to all that is possible in the supervisory relationship. The supervisee will present all that he/she knows or thinks he/she knows about the problem. I will soon begin to introduce my tools of the trade, action methods and drama, to facilitate the exploration of what is present. Time, impatience, emotional intensity and the pressing need for solutions remain suspended as we forge ahead into uncharted territory. The goal is not to fix, correct, improve, change. It is simply to raise awareness.

Michael is completing his training in dramatherapy and has been seeing Brenda individually for over 20 sessions. Brenda is a 45-year-old professional woman, married with two children who have left home, and she is feeling utterly depressed and lonely. In her therapy so far she has explored her earlier feelings of abandonment in adolescence and her usual methods of coping by assuming extreme responsibility for others. She is now at a point of impasse in her therapy with Michael. Unmoved and unmoving, Brenda presents herself as weak, immobilized by the terror of being alone now that she's discovered her husband has betrayed her with another woman.

Michael comes to supervision claiming he is stuck. 'How do we move on? I am just standing there. I don't know what we're doing or where we are going.' He shows me a drawing Brenda made in their last session. She drew herself fat and alone behind a desk, while the rest of her family grouped together opposite her at the other end of the page.

What do you see in the drawing? I ask Michael.

She has taken a ruling position in the family. She is like a boss behind a desk. She takes care of them. But she is overeating (her usual method of coping with her depression in adolescence) and alone. The family are there but not connected to her.

How do you connect to her right now? I ask him. I want to help Michael explore his current state more intently so I offer him the possibility to physicalize his relationship to Brenda in the space, using his body as well as objects.

Michael creates a long, thin line on the floor using a sari. He places himself on one side of the cloth and places a stool on the other, to represent Brenda as a little girl. He stands, holding out his hand.

Speak to Brenda freely, I encourage him.

> I feel angry and weak. I am pulling you by the hand, to take you places but you don't come near me, you look elsewhere.

What are you aware of right now? I ask him.

> She gives me a familiar role and I take it. She pretends to be weak, but I know she isn't.

What do you want to do right now?

> I feel the urge to go back and get her to pull me instead.

I note the change in Michael's energy and decide to capitalize on it. I invite Michael to change roles and be Brenda pulling him. I am hoping that embodying the client will enlighten Michael on Brenda's motivation and needs.

Michael (as Brenda):

> I need you to be here but my mind is racing left and right. I don't know what I need. I feel the air is hollow. As if my body is weightless. You will go away too. Why should I invest in you? I want to look after you. I feel obliged. We are too close somehow.

After his experience of Brenda in role, I invite Michael to return to his original position as himself while I hold the role of

Brenda and repeat her lines to him. Afterwards I ask him what he is aware of now. We have unpacked some of the dynamics of the interaction between them and I want to give Michael an opportunity to reflect on the process.

> I get stronger when she weakens. It's like she is bribing me, or giving me gifts. She wants some distance. I, however, want the closeness. I realize that my own expectations for intimacy with her stop me and the therapy. She needs distance. I can't save her, I can't be responsible for her, I can't make her do things. I feel relieved. I know what I'm doing.

Michael experienced a significant shift in his perspective on his client. He'd entered the supervision session not knowing what he was doing and exited with new insight. The enactment and exploration of what was present for him allowed him to explore more fully all his feelings, projections, intuitions and judgments about his client and reach a new level of awareness about the subtle game of manipulations that kept him and Brenda stuck in the familiar role of being a child parent. After this supervision session Michael felt free to explore new interventions in his relationship to Brenda and continue the process of therapy with renewed interest and inspiration.

Both Michael and his client (or his perception thereof) experienced rigidity, a fixed Gestalt in other words. Michael came to me having realized that his interaction with Brenda had become repetitive, dull and, like stagnant waters, highly toxic. Their system of relating was inevitably changing, but not in therapeutically viable ways. Brenda was getting worse and Michael was feeling useless and despondent. My intervention consisted in raising Michael's awareness but why use drama to achieve this? Michael could have simply written a report of his therapeutic assessment of the client or told me his current situation in words. This would constitute 'telling me and seeing what is there'. But would this have been enough? Evidently not. Michael 'knew' something was wrong but he also 'knew' he couldn't fix it because he couldn't exactly pinpoint it. He knew that he didn't know but didn't quite know *what* he didn't know. The reader may forgive me if I sound like a zen monk but I would like to refer to my beloved T.S. Eliot to elucidate my viewpoint. In *East Coker*, Eliot (1944) writes 'In order to arrive at what you do not know you must go by a way which is the way of ignorance'. I encourage the reader to read the full poem to appreciate the compatibility between Eliot's ideas and quantum physics, particularly the uncertainty principle of Heisenberg. The poet urges us to accept that the only way to achieve any concrete awareness of anything knowable is to become familiar with the idea of not knowing. This applies not only to our awareness of things in the world but also, and perhaps most fundamentally, to our own sense of self. Ownership, knowledge and self identity, therefore, are fluid processes that one becomes aware of through their absence, a *via negativa* which leads to the transcendent paradox of reaching your being by what you are not and owning what you do not have. I regard this process as the main road, the central avenue to change. It runs through contact with the other, whether this is our very own hitherto unknown self, or our client, or supervisee.

Where does this knowledge of the unknown reside, that Eliot so evocatively intimates? Michael's example showed that the knowledge existed in his brain, but out of conscious awareness. Cognitivists would say that the knowledge was in his right hemisphere but Michael's dominant left hemisphere, capable of reasoned thought and elaborate analysis, had no access to it (Watzlawick 1981). His right brain, capable of symbolic thought, metaphorical expression, imaginative speculation and intuitive knowledge, possessed some valuable answers that remained out of reach. In my supervisory capacity I performed the work of a brain surgeon. I momentarily cut off

Michael's corpus callosum which connects the two brain hemi-spheres and gave him the opportunity to access his right brain. I did this by engaging him in drama. My simple prompt to be Brenda and speak as her led Michael away from his fixed left brain version of reality and into the world of possibilities hiding in the folds of his right cortex. After the experience of being Brenda, Michael could not unlearn what he had learned. Back in his own skin, with his corpus callosum restored, Michael 'knew' his client and his relationship to her in a changed way.

The shift from unknowing to knowing, from defeat to strength, from despondency to hope occurs during a thrilling moment of discovery which imbues the supervisory process with energy, creativity and power. Playful engagement with action methods demarcates the field of inquiry and offers the structure wherein exploration can evolve. I am always careful, however, not to impose forms and exercises but rather work with the supervisee to find the apposite structure which may facilitate their experience. As I am temperamentally rather impatient, I make a concerted effort to remain detached and not rush to fix any issue before the supervisee is entirely ready to connect with his/her new insight. I mostly rely on stories, myths, images and symbols to assist my supervisees in accessing their right brain awareness, especially if they come to supervision presenting cognitive blocks.

However, raising awareness is not so straightforward a task. There are instances when 'stuckness' is revealed both in the therapist–client relationship and the supervisor–supervisee relationship. This parallel process can often escape my awareness and I, as a result, err in intensifying my supervisee's impasse by circumventing the obvious. The blocks to awareness are many, both for the supervisor and the supervisee, and it is common knowledge that what we often find most difficult to see is what is right in front of us. I learned from experience that the easiest route to awareness in such cases is not necessarily through promoting right brain insight, but by engaging in direct action. This way, immediate, spontaneous contact with the other person inevitably leads somewhere else and shakes both parties' perceptions.

The following example illustrates this: Katherine is a young counsellor who attends my monthly supervision group. For a number of sessions she has been bringing to supervision her difficulties in relating to clients who overwhelm her, make her feel small and ineffectual and often resist her interventions. Katherine is very pretty, dresses fashionably and has a very youthful air about her. Her clients are mainly older women who are often expressing doubt about her ability to understand their plight and help them. Katherine feels that her clients patronize her and question her authority.

For a number of sessions we have been exploring her concerns in a group context, by using metaphors and symbolic play. Katherine gains awareness of the dynamics of her relationship to her clients but she still feels stuck and as time progresses, her discomfort intensifies. I am obviously not grasping something. During our last session, Katherine presented her situation in an elaborate drawing which clearly showed the amount of confusion she still experiences. She drew two chairs facing each other to represent her and her client. Above them she drew a vast cloud of unspoken fantasies, fears, doubts and secrets that contaminate the contact between the two people. The relationship between them remained largely in a chaotic web of speculation where nothing was clearly articulated.

I invited Katherine to speak about her image. She proceeded to give a protracted explanation of how she doesn't know what's going on, how she cannot assert her authority with her client and how she fears that she keeps getting more and more confused about her client's often unconnected ramblings as she avoids stopping her to ask for clarification for fear of being a directive therapist. Trying to be non-directive she refrained from spontaneously interacting with her client. Katherine spoke for a long time, explaining, analysing, reflecting, reassessing, re-evaluating but basically staying stuck in her own rhetoric. I equally began to feel that her logic was impenetrable and I couldn't think of what to say to help her.

I became aware of physical discomfort. I started getting nauseous, dizzy and began to feel utterly confused myself. I noticed how I embarked on flights of fancy, imagining possible reasons why Katherine spoke in that manner. I started fantasizing about Katherine's consulting room and what went on in there. I began to imagine her client's home life and very soon I was immersed in a fantasy world from which it would have been impossible to escape had the sense of discomfort in my body not been so intense. Stop! I shouted at Katherine in desperation. She looked at me in stunned silence. During the pregnant pause which followed I had my epiphany: Katherine was doing to me what the client did to her.

> What are you doing right now? I asked Katherine.
> I am listening to you. I am looking at you.
> How do I look to you? Are you doubting me?
> No! You look 'substantial'. You are here.
> Do you question my authority?
> No. On the contrary. I am interested in what you want to say to me.
> Am I being directive?
> No, you are being interested. I get it!

In his book *Laws of Form*, G. Spencer Brown (1973) writes about the limits of representation in communication. Certain forms of experience cannot be translated into descriptive language. Like the taste of a cake, we cannot literally describe it. The best we can do is offer the reader a series of commands that will lead her to experience the taste. It's called a cake recipe

(Watzlawick 1981). Katherine, after my command to stop talking, became thoughtful and vastly more aware of her experience with her client than any of my previous attempts had achieved. She resolved to try and be more direct. She began to change her old belief about what a directive therapist was. She ceased associating the construct of directiveness with the idea of interrupting her client to ask for clarification. Conversely, I realized how seduced I unconsciously became by her belief that being a person-centred counsellor meant letting the client ramble on ad nauseam. By staying on the here and now level of my relationship to Katherine I observed my physical reaction to her and acted accordingly. I also gained awareness and by doing so, altered my form of interaction. This intervention had the domino effect of raising Katherine's awareness and, naturally, altering her behaviour too.

Using my whole body to listen, observe and be present in front of my supervisee, as I did with Katherine, opens up additional inroads to understanding and creative release of ideas. Sometimes action, the moment of choice, is facilitated by attending to what Eugene Gendlin calls the 'felt sense' (Gendlin 1980). The 'felt sense' is a cue derived from the body, a pinch in the heart, a flutter in the stomach, a sudden headache, something which can be used effectively in supervision as a vital instrument and catalyst for change. Gendlin, a phenomenologist par excellence, in his seminal book *Focusing* offers steps to a process of coming into awareness of the physical component of an experience. In my view, the most important step is first staying with one's body and waiting for the felt sense to appear fully, welcoming it and allowing it to emerge. The next step is to connect the felt sense with words, images and further physical sensations. This process allows the supervisor as well as the supervisee to access their experience not from the cognitive plane, which often leads to stuckness, but from an intuitive, physically informed and imaginative perspective. Attending to the felt sense may not assist the supervisee in finding solutions to problems like how to find consulting rooms in a new town, but can be very beneficial in helping him/her cope with resistance or resolve feelings of despondency when running a difficult group or exploring the supervision relationship itself, as in the following case:

Deborah is a very experienced counselor in her sixties, who became a therapist after a long career as a social worker. Despite the wealth of experience she possesses, she is timid and withdrawn in the supervision group and avoids bringing her own casework for discussion. When this was brought to her awareness, she became defensive: 'I just don't feel I have anything to work through. I learn most by observing others'. My curiosity is why she isn't using the supervision group to the maximum. What is stopping her from making full use of a service offered to her? What is stopping her from making valuable contributions to the group? I invited her to attend to her felt sense. She reported a sunken feeling in the heart. She stayed a long time with this sense, letting it expand inside her body. When I invited her to connect it to a word, she came up with the word 'jealousy'. When she held the felt sense and the word together, images of her early childhood in a home for disadvantaged children emerged. 'I've always had to compete with other children for the attention of a mother figure,' Deborah admits tearfully. 'I've been in supervision groups before but always with male supervisors. This is different. You are my "mum". I feel the same insecurity now as I did back then.' This is a sensitive and powerful issue for Deborah. Shaking her old patterns may take a long time, but having recognized it she is now openly sharing it in the group and exploring it in her own therapy.

Passion for change is, to me, synonymous with passion for life as process. This can practically pose some difficult challenges, such as how to stay open and patient with what's not fully articulated and known. Starting from a position of curiosity can help me keep the inquiry going and allows me the openness to explore various avenues and possibilities, as I demonstrate in Michael's case. Ultimately I believe the supervisee possesses all his/her answers in the folds of his/her right or left cortex or the soft tissue of the belly but isn't confident enough to trust his/her competence. I see it as my job to make the supervisee aware of his/her competence and often see myself as the person who shakes the carpet. In other words, I help supervisees change by assisting them in questioning their belief systems and checking tacit assumptions, expectations and points of interest. Einstein famously retorted to Heisenberg that theory defines what we can observe (Watzlawick 1981), thus showing that awareness is a matter of setting conceptual boundaries rather than a matter of intelligence or capability. Katherine's as well as Deborah's examples illustrate how unconscious and unquestioned beliefs may contaminate or hamper both the therapeutic and the supervisory relationship.

In my mind passion, fascination and desire for exploration all inevitably share the same foundation: a keen interest in the unknown, or the not-yet-fully-known, the mysterious, the promising, the pulsating quantum moment when all things are possible. Supervision has so far been a bright candle to life as change and transformation, as well as a wide platform for learning and integrating all my experiences and knowledge in order to help others see, learn and grow. I've come a long way and, yes, the place looks comfortably new and strangely familiar. But it's not the same. Thankfully.

References

Brown, G.S. (1973) *Laws of Form*. New York: Bantam Books.

Capra, F. (1996) *The Web of Life: A New Scientific Understanding of Living Systems*. New York: Anchor Books.

Eliot, T.S. (1944) *Four Quartets*. London: Faber and Faber.

Gendlin, E.T. (1980) *Focusing: A Tool for Changing Times*. New York: Bantam Books.

Perls, F. (1973) *The Gestalt Approach*. Palo Alto, CA: Science and Behavior Books.

Perls, F., Hefferline, R.F. and Goodman, P. (1951) *Gestalt Therapy*. New York: Dell.

Watzlawick, P. (1981) *The Language of Change. Elements of Therapeutic Communication*. New York: Basic Books.

Winnicott, D.W. (1971) *Playing and Reality*. London: Tavistock Publications.

Introduction to Chapter 9

I met Jane comparatively recently, and was struck by how much she wanted to bring spiritual values into education. She is very committed to the importance of reflection in which she has engaged for all of her working life. She describes her lifelong journey in education and supervision, and argues convincingly how giving space to teachers will free the passion to learn in students.

When I asked Jane what she wanted the reader to know about her chapter she said:

> That there is rich and hopeful territory in the often unexplored, unexpressed 'gap' in aspects of the communication between teachers and their pupils. What makes me passionate about this work is that when teachers are given dedicated time to reflect on what they do in classrooms they can address and inhabit this 'gap' as a place where they can be even more in touch with what the students need in relationship to them and how learning together, beyond the gap, can then become a real and fulfilling possibility.

Chapter 9

Freeing the Passion to Learn
Jane Reed

In this chapter I tell the story of how I have woken up to the power of supervision in my life and developed it in my work. It describes how I have connected learning, passion and supervision through my encounters in a range of 'supervisory' settings. Over a 30-year period I have come to see the ways in which 'teaching' can either serve or undermine learning in classroom settings and how important it is for teachers and school leaders to take the opportunity for supervision if they are to free the passion to learn in their pupils.

Introduction

Bert Hellinger (2002) observed: 'In the seed form, the whole is already is at work, yet without being fully present' (p.55).

I have a very clear memory of my first encounter with supervision and its passionate possibilities. It was 15 February 1972. I was sitting looking at a book of photographs put together by Henri Nouwen. I was almost 22 and about to take my final undergraduate exams. Nouwen had published this wordless book to support meditation practice. I remember vividly turning the pages and gazing at the photos of people in different situations and from many cultures; they were giving birth, fighting, being lovers, playing with their children. Through these pictures on that afternoon my world and my place in it suddenly expanded. The memory is of a sense of joy, awe, a part for me to play in the Universe; of being connected to everyone and they to me. Now I realize that I had stood for the first time, that I remember consciously, in the bigger Me. It was quite overwhelming and had a dizzy, disturbing effect for days and months afterwards.

I date the beginning of my adult political and spiritual journey to that afternoon. I associate this biographical fragment from 35 years ago with becoming passionate about and involved in supervision and passionate about it both as supervisor and as supervisee. My introduction to it was what was called at my Church of England College 'spiritual direction'. The context was simple but precipitant: the Chaplain gave me Nouwen's book to read as he ran to answer the phone. The experience prompted an encounter with the relationship between myself and a source of inspiration and love that I have been finding, losing and following ever since. My reflection now is that it was a more profound connection with my passion than I had had in my life to that point. Another, more analytic observation is that this encounter was a stimulus for the development of the inner world of a prospective teacher trying to leave home, grow up and find out what her life was going to be about.

I have often thought about what the Chaplain did as a 'supervisor' when I go back to that memory. He responded to a need, was present to the need and supported me in putting what I was feeling into a bigger picture, a larger whole. *Response, presence, support* and *connection*; those are the words that come to mind now. This process and the interconnection of its four strands helped me to make sense of my experience. Realizing that my experience could become a friend and resource, not a source of anxiety was somehow what freed my passion and this I can see now is the core of what it means to learn.

Sustaining my passion through supervision has become a source of nourishment. It has come in the telling and reframing of my journey and the journeys of my clients using those four elements. It has come in a world of ever-changing contexts and commitments: making sense of being and becoming, especially in professional contexts. A central point of this story is that the Chaplain recommended a book called *The Casework Relationship* written by an American Jesuit, Felix P. Biestek. I have it still on my shelf, and went back to it while starting to write this chapter. The foundations he explores were all part of the context of my own formation in the field of human relations that was emerging at that time in the 1970s. There was a connection between the spiritual and the supervisory, an ever-evolving relationship which makes the latter passionate and sustains my work as a supervisor.

How I came to be working in the field

I studied for an MA in education early in my career and part of the reason for doing that was to continue to get the sort of support I had had at my training college. I remember how supported I felt by the tutors at the university. This was in stark contrast to the climate in the school I was teaching at, where there was only contact with colleagues if you were struggling, or had time to be in the staff room for a cup of coffee. We had a staff meeting to discuss routine matters once a week. The head teacher mostly stayed in his office and an inspector visited me once during my first year of teaching and signed me off as being able to teach. While I did feel passionate about the children, I felt beleaguered and alone in the classroom. As a young teacher experiencing this culture from the 'other side' for the first time I was getting some insight into why my own teachers had seemed so unavailable and defended. It was as though we as pupils had to be on our best behaviour, get the answers right and speak only when spoken to in order to keep something rather fragile in place for them. No wonder learning felt like hard work and not anything very passionate.

I was busy at the time of studying for my MA, reading and studying the writing of Lawrence Stenhouse on the topic of teacher development and what came to be known in the trade as 'reflective and collegial practice'. I tried for my thesis, somewhat counter-culturally, to reflect, research and write about my practice in my classroom of seven-year-olds. I came to see from my own experience how impossible it was to do that by myself. I ended up in my thesis describing why I couldn't do what I intended to do! In the process I gained some real insights into the process of change needed to enable schools to be places where teachers can learn too. I began to see that there needed to be a culture of openness and reciprocity, a willingness to put practice under scrutiny and to support each other in the process; to encourage each other to work from a place where we could sustain passionate contact with children and enable real learning to happen. I took a big professional and promotional leap and went to work at Hackney Teachers' Centre. I wasn't quite sure what I would find there but I was determined to find for teachers, especially those new to the profession, a way to feel supported and to reflect on their practice in non-threatening ways, to enable their head teachers and local authority to help provide those opportunities.

That was where almost immediately I discovered the Tavistock Clinic's emerging work in work-based consultation. It was a period of enormous growth and amazing opportunity for me that I grabbed instinctively. The Inner London

Education Authority was innovative, it had the opportunity to be, and I am thankful for the learning I did at that time. It had set up one of the first projects of its kind, which was to build three teams of three teachers to work in schools alongside teachers in Hackney classrooms to develop the curriculum. The fact that they were to be classroom-based was part of an emerging recognition that teachers needed support to develop their practice. The support of a team member was not to be seen as a deficit approach, but as a mentor to discuss practice and work alongside the teacher with the children and provide expertise and experience.

Denise Taylor, a senior clinical psychologist, worked with us in the project and that was my first experience of being in a group where as a project team we were supported in thinking not just about what individuals were doing but also how this was part of the social and cultural dynamics of each school. We learnt to think, to respond rather than just react in each other's presence, to really listen. We began to see what each team member could get caught up in if they weren't very clear about the task and the boundaries of their role. We examined conflicting issues for the teams if they were to succeed in helping the schools and then to leave them to stand on their own.

My role became one of running the weekly support group for the nine team members who would present their work and we as a group had a confidential space to reflect on it, its meaning and the next steps for the teams. We looked at the dynamics in teams, between teams and between the teams and the schools. This was my first real introduction to supervision/coaching work. I went to the Westminster Pastoral Foundation for some training in counselling skills. Looking back I realize what pioneering work they were doing in studying the relationship between theology and human relations as an emerging field. I became fascinated by Jungian approaches to the unconscious, the archetypes and human development. I can look back and see the part that the writing of books such as the pastoral book recommended by my Chaplain was playing in the development of the emerging human relations field.

For several years we held a weekly staff support group at Hackney Teachers' Centre based on the Tavistock model and run by trainee consultants on Denise Taylor's course. I went on to do this course part-time for two years in the mid-1980s. While I was leading Hackney Teachers' Centre, I was in weekly supervision for the first time. Barrie, a local social worker and trainee family therapist, was my supervisor. Barrie introduced me to systemic approaches that just made so much sense. I learnt to become a systemic thinker and his care and coaching helped me to develop a style as a systemic coach. It was in this period that I added to my model of response, presence, support and connection *the school as a whole system, the context of the whole system, system defences* and *projections.* Coaching takes place in a context that will be affecting the client as they carry material from the whole organization and become part of the 'loyalty' system of the school. I added to my training portfolio some time in group analytic training and therapy and very significant work with the Grubb Institute on the process of organizational role analysis in schools. We began there the first group relations event to study the teaching and learning process in the workplace. This background and training has sustained me and enabled me to keep passionate first about pupils and their learning, and second about the coaching that is needed for classrooms and schools to enable learning to take place.

What I want to do in the rest of this chapter is to describe the approach to my practice as it has developed over the past 30 years. I draw on biographical material to trace the roots and values in my own development. I reflect on my experience of being a client in work-based supervision and try to illustrate the connection between supervision and school and teacher development that I have been making in my work. I use examples from my current practice to illustrate what is passionate about this way of working. I want to suggest that releasing the passion to learn is a fundamental task for a school and that educators who are free and available to their students can act from their passion. They need space however to reflect, to get support and to talk about their work: *to experience response, presence, support and connection.*

The context of my current work? After 22 years in classrooms, a Teacher Development Centre in inner London and as a Local Authority Adviser I have been working in the Higher Education sector for 12 years as a lecturer, consultant and coach in the field of school and teacher development. Throughout my career I have trained in and developed a variety of systemic and psychodynamic approaches to consultancy, supervision and group work. Educators tend not to refer to supervision in the same way that those with a social care background do, but the coaching and mentoring we do I am sure has a similar function, if practised in different ways. I will therefore refer to coaching or consulting as my work except where I am drawing on examples where the relationship was described as a supervisory one. I remain I hope within the paradigm of supervision explored in this book.

The context for supervision/coaching in education

The classroom is the place where the heart of a school should beat the loudest. Its learning heartbeat in reality is often only heard in a muted way. I am not sure where my fascination with classrooms as a social setting came from. In one way or another I have been in them all my life and they are a source of fascination and frustration both to me and the several hundred teachers I have worked with and whose daily job it is to be there. A source of insight for me about the classroom as a place of learning came as I confronted my own experience as a summer born (therefore young in the year group) child in the infant school I went to, which was not particularly positive. The teachers I encountered as a child seemed mostly terrifying, judging, shaming and controlling women. My mother had been told at the end of the first week of my being at school, when I was just five, 'Well she doesn't know very much.' I secretly continue to heal the wound that hearing that remark caused me and deal with the lack of respect that was accorded to me as a young learner. It took me a long time to really experience my own intelligence and believe from the inside that I had some.

Classrooms are many things but for the most part they are not glamorous places. They do not come that high on the list of research priorities in organizations like mine. Occasionally I find a story that contradicts that sense. As I write I come from a visit to a downtown elementary school in Boston, Massachusetts where Lucy and her colleague David, a professor at Boston College, have set up a project called the Mindful Teacher Project. This is in contrast to the Marxist notion of 'alienated work' (in this case teaching).

During our conversations Lucy told me that her work in the classroom is never done, that she could study and complete 12 doctoral qualifications but this would never quite equip her to be able to achieve what she would like to each day with her pupils. She talked about the feelings of inadequacy and self-doubt she and her colleagues face. Why, she asked me, should she end the day feeling bad about herself when she puts heart and soul into her pupils' learning and well-being? The Mindful Teacher Project has been set up to provide a space for teachers to meet, reflect, share their issues together and gain insight into what they are experiencing: to re-experience their passion. Urban teachers across the globe experience the same thing; often under pressure they need to find the resources to stay in the classrooms where the heartbeat of their schools beats the loudest.

Lucy articulated so well why there is a need for work-based consulting and coaching in education. There was no doubt at all that she feels passionate about the pupils that she teaches and what she wants for them. For teachers to be *responsive*, *present*, *supportive* and *making connections* for their pupils they need to be able to draw on resources that are often invisible. What I have noticed time and time again is that unless they are resourced to *think* about their work and how it makes them feel they feel overwhelmed or defend against the task of connecting to their pupils. They are resourced as soon as they can have an experience of the forces that keep a distance between themselves and the pupils. When they can also develop insight into what is at work in the school as a whole that may be cluttering their best intentions, then they can mobilize and draw on their passion more freely. Institutional life so easily takes us away from the ground of being where our passion originates.

It remains a challenge for educational innovation that despite the vast amount of funding that has been directed at schools by governments in the western world during the past two decades the classroom as an operational unit can still feel like a lonely and stressful place to work, especially if you are under pressure to produce so called 'results' for which you feel personally accountable. The literature that has been written about professional learning for teachers in the last 30 years suggests that teachers flourish when they can find space to reflect on their practice, learn with and from each other and have enough opportunity to talk about what they are doing and what concerns them. This also needs to be heard and respected as an important source of feedback by their leaders and managers. Transforming what is known in the trade as the 'egg crate culture' is what school development and change is all about. Classrooms need to be connected to each other and so do their teachers. This can then enable them to be as available as they possibly can for their pupils and in that relationship free up the passion to learn that is the joint endeavour of the learning and teaching relationship.

Current practice

My work in the last 20 years has been to try to integrate and use this foundational learning and perspective in the field and to build my own practice from the eclectic base that I come out of. While owing a lot to my psychodynamic roots, which often enable me to sense and work with unnameable dynamics with and for clients, I have come full circle to a more Rogerian, humanistic–spiritual base to my work which always plays attention to the systemic factors at work and is based now in the new positive psychology as well as phenomenology. I owe a great deal more recently to the work of Bert Hellinger and the field of family and organizational constellations.

While preparing for this chapter, I came across a reference in my Grubb Institute notes from the early 1990s that said 'Why are we so conditioned to undervalue the resources of pupils?' This struck a chord with the work that I have been developing since I came back to join the staff at the Institute of Education. As I mentioned earlier, education in England has been through a time of enormous change with billions of pounds pumped into multiple initiatives. Schools have had to learn to be held to account for their performance results. While there have been some benefits to all of this in the form of higher standards in literacy and numeracy in particular and more accountability, transparency and evaluation, this period has led to a tendency for instrumental, short-term solutions, a constant wondering when the inspectors will call and a dependency on externally driven approaches. In addition I find my clients 'punch drunk' on action and anxiety that is increasingly driven, with almost no time at all to think, their focus almost exclusively on the pupils' performance rather than their learning. Releasing the passion to learn remains an urgent priority for the system as a whole.

While the resources of the pupils are paid lip service to in such initiatives as listening to the student 'voices', they are quite ignored in other ways. It is quite common to hear the question 'How shall we drill down to the pupils' level to see what the impact is of this (or that) initiative?' Though ugly, I think this sentiment probably reflects a truth. It is as if the pupils have had so many reforms piled on top of them that they are waiting patiently in the dark under belly of their schools for us to reach them. My colleague Caroline and I were processing some observations about what makes a school focus on learning the other day. She observed: 'The adults are in this school because the children are and the children are there because the adults are.' This kind of relational stance is a step on the road to freeing the passion to learn.

Two current examples

My work takes me into supervision and coaching in a broad sense; sometimes with individuals, sometimes with groups. Sometimes in contexts that are more training based, others that have the express purpose of being consultancy. Currently I am working with three schools: the middle leaders in one and the senior team in the other two. The models for the work vary. One has been for two initial, three-hour sessions with some follow-up in the next term, the other an ongoing termly meeting. We meet where there is a space on the school site, which itself can be an issue. Many schools do not have adult learning spaces other than the staff room. The task they give me usually is to develop their effectiveness as a team. Together we begin to construct the agenda by their telling me about their experience of the school, their roles and working together. What it is that is troubling them takes longer to untangle. This is the first way they experience my *response* as well as my *presence* as I listen in the fullest way possible, ask questions that help build the big picture, their sense of the system and context in which they operate. Bit by bit we piece it together and I usually map it visually as we go, or if there is time I invite them to do their own pictures and share them with each other. I have often asked myself: am I wasting my clients' time as I seek to find out in detail about their reality? I have come to trust that they have rarely if ever had the chance to talk about their experience in a work session and never with each other. The work in the staff meetings they do have is either business, discussing reports or managing the latest initiative. It is rarely space to *think and reflect about their professional practice.* They always report relief and pleasure at the opportunity to really hear what each other has to say.

They tell me that they are more confident to provide reflective space for each other as a result of the work that we do together and to discuss what is really happening for them rather than what they think others will want to hear. My sense is that their response and presence for each other begins to grow. In this first stage of mapping the whole picture they will often present issues or initiatives they are dealing with as separate unrelated fragments. I have learnt from Peter Senge's writing about systems thinking, that exposing the mental models in use and enabling clients to see each others' and then to build a systemic picture that reflects their joint reality can be very effective as a tool to develop more *connected* practices. Helping them to see the relation between bits of the system that otherwise they experience as separate is a key part of what we do. The effect seems to release them from some kind of foggy dependency and capacity to be more strategic. The pupils become a more central part of what they talk about and what they are building solutions for.

In another setting I am working with Helen, a colleague who is responsible for developing aspects of the 'Every Child Matters' agenda. We have developed a model of joint supervision. There is quite a task to develop settings that have the full range of educational facilities as well as care for the children and multi-agency working for the families. The model we are using is one we are developing together. Helen was a former client so I know her well. We between us have a pretty clear grasp of the issues facing our clients. We have been working with Kathryn and Sonia for several sessions, building the big picture with them, getting a sense of what they face and the dynamics they experience in the staff team. They too are clearly passionate about their work for the children. Sometimes managing the staff, especially into new roles and relationships, can feel really daunting. They seem to really benefit from the joint work and also from seeing Helen in between sessions.

We sense after the second session that while Kathryn is *responding* to us, she isn't quite *present* in the sessions. She often seems agitated and overwhelmed, not far from tears. We sense that something is getting in the way of her passion and that her confidence needs to surface. We feel a bit concerned about her when we reflect on the session. Somehow we know we need to trust, that we need to continue to *respond*, be *present* and to *support* her to allow whatever needs to join us in the session. In the next session she is very concerned about two staff that are not getting on. After listening to the story and knowing she is resourced with our support we gently ask her to *make the connection* with her own experience. She starts to sob. She is eventually able to tell us about a time in the workplace where she was bullied and could not get any support. She had never felt that she had been able to communicate with anyone her experience of this trauma. She was clearly still living the pain and distress this had caused her and trying to keep it suppressed as it tried to bubble up into the light of day. She was ashamed to cry in the session; we tried to reassure her that it was the best thing possible for her work that this issue had surfaced. It was interfering with her sense of herself as a manager and her own capacity to be present and respond appropriately.

In the next session we didn't refer back, thinking she would have done so if she needed to. Kathryn seemed so much brighter, more confident and more in charge. We had provided a safe space where the memory of her experience could emerge and stay inside the boundary of our supervisory work, but the border between this work and the therapeutic is a fine one. Kathryn's passion for learning is palpable now and she seems so much more present and alive in the sessions. She has committed herself to a new programme of professional learning. There is something about her degree of centredness now in herself that has enabled her to be present to staff in a renewed way and she reported that the staff are more present to the children than they have been.

Learning from my own supervision

I have been in and out of supervision, training and therapy throughout my career and it was not that long ago after a break, that I found myself a new supervisor and recommitted to the work of being in supervision. I had been studying organizational constellations and saw things in the role I had in my day job that I needed to get clarity about. I meet Jenny about every six weeks for two hours and we have developed a ritual of including a shared lunch in the session while we work. This may run counter to some orthodoxies but it works for us! I have shared the intentions of this bit of writing with her and we reflected together on the work that we have been doing. I reminded her that she began by inviting me to share my values for my professional life with her. Of course there is overlap with my personal values too. In 30 years of working life I don't think I had ever discussed what I stand for, really.

My values have been in formation or implicit or not really ever arisen as a topic to focus on. It seemed obvious to me that communication, an empathic stance, a belief in people's fundamental goodness and trusting and connecting to our feelings were the basis of being an educator and facilitator.

Jenny's real interest in my values and how they affect my thinking and style as a supervisor/coach has been very influential. Also the way she relates to me, which she describes beautifully as 'attunement', is taking me further down the road I am on in this phase of my career. It has been a long haul from that first illuminatory experience in my chaplain's sitting room. For of course this story about the process of developing supervision for others has also been my story. In the Constellations community I belong to (based on the work of Bert Hellinger) I am also training in systemic approaches to coaching. We discuss the need that we have 'To Help' and how this can be constructed by us as help that is needed by our clients even though it can get in the way of the task. Jenny has worked with me on this issue in a very supportive way. She meets me and is teaching me anew about how to meet others and to be a reflective presence rather than to try and help. Because we have both been involved in learning about constellations based on the work of Bert Hellinger, we know that our time together takes place in a special space, that the gift of confidential uninterrupted time is the chance to be alert together to the field energies of the situations and issues I bring from my work. To allow these invisible and visible forces to show themselves and re-align for the resourcing of my clients and myself is a very passionate business. I leave the sessions with fire in my soul!

Perhaps I am ready now to really be met in supervision, to be available to myself, to experience greater intimacy with the universal energies I know to be supporting me. At least I am getting better at it, accessing those resources of *response, presence, support* and *making connections.* As a result of working with Jenny I now see supervision as a space where a new environment can be created that supervisees feel in charge of and where they can in partnership with their supervisor strive for better solutions. In the process they can get more in touch with their own congruence with their working situation and this leads to a more centred sense of themselves that releases and unclutters the passion to learn.

Acknowledgements

I would like to acknowledge the many inspirational clients, teachers, friends and colleagues who have travelled on this path with me, particularly my supervisor Jenny Colls.

Reference

Hellinger, B. (2002) *On Life and Other Paradoxes.* Phoenix, AZ: Zeig, Tucker and Theisen.

Introduction to Chapter 10

And so finally my chapter. In it I am wanting to show how all our beliefs about how the world 'should be' seem to give us protection but in fact keep us in a state of fear by not allowing us to be in the present. Presence, nowness, are themes that run through the book. In many ways this chapter seemed to me to come full circle with Jochen's chapter because we both want to challenge some deeply held cultural assumptions, and see supervision as a place to do this.

I asked myself what I wanted the reader to get from reading my chapter and I replied:

> To see the spirituality in supervision, especially for me in group supervision where we can act as one body working together in the service of what is being brought. I would also like them to know how much I struggle with keeping my heart open in the face of fear, and how supervision has helped me in that process.

Chapter 10

Fear and Love In
and Beyond Supervision
Robin Shohet

Fear knocked at the door. Love answered and there was no-one there. (Sufi maxim)

In this chapter I am inviting the reader to look at how fear and love might enter the supervisory relationship. Fear can pose sometimes as anxiety, anger, shame, preoccupation with safety, rigid adherence to beliefs, rules and procedures. These are defences that are rarely useful and keep us separated. I believe that fear covers love, a love that is not ephemeral, but the naturally compassionate essence of who we are. Passionate supervision offers a space to bring fear into consciousness and dissolve it so we can enter into a space where loving presence can bring healing for supervisor, supervisee and client. Numerous examples are given, taken especially from group supervision.

Introduction

One of the reasons I am passionate about supervision stems from my first experience of supervision as a residential social worker. The sessions were so supportive, challenging and full of love, that 30 years later I am still filled with gratitude.

Working to support individuals and teams in their demanding work is a way of passing on this gratitude.

I see fear and love as central to a supervisor's work. We have very deep needs to connect, and fear gets in our way. It is the biggest block to intimacy and communication. If we can manage intimacy, and the fears around it in supervision, then this will pass on to our supervisees and our clients.

Sheila Ryan, one of the contributors to this book, writes:

> Fear is born in the mind. It lives in the body and keeps us separated from ourselves – and so from each other. (Personal communication)

Most of the following chapter will be about fear. Love, like the sun, is always there, but it is covered by the clouds of fear. Exposing the fear in order to dissolve it is one of the routes to love. It is because fear is often so difficult to spot that I concentrate initially on fear. In the following example of a dream I had while thinking about this chapter, I am angry and do not initially recognize the fear behind it.

I am sitting on a lawn with two students – I am in some teaching capacity. One of them has a laptop and the other asks if he or she will look something up for them on the internet. The one with the computer says, 'Certainly not. If I get it wrong you will sue me.' I get very angry and say, 'It is remarks like that that perpetuate the fear culture. If friends can't help each other, we are in a mad world, full of fear.' I wake up and it takes me a few moments to realize how much I am part of the fear culture. My anger in the dream masks a fear about what is happening in the world around the fear of being sued.

In that way the dream is not simply personal. We live in a culture that promotes fear. I recognize this in my dream, but I am frightened of fear, and hide this with a challenge, some anger. As supervisors and supervisees, I would like us to be aware of how to recognize and use the fear creatively. We can so easily become part of passing on the fear driven norms of society, instead of daring to stand outside them – even for a moment. Supervision offers us the opportunity to bring our defences, the norms we have introjected, into awareness, and gives us the chance to free up our passion rather than be herded into a respectable orthodoxy.

Core beliefs

At the heart of my work as a supervisor is examining core beliefs. These are beliefs which we see as self-evident, fundamental truths. They can be about the world, human nature, ourselves, our profession, about how people should or shouldn't behave. They usually involve the right/wrong polarity. We think anyone who disagrees with these beliefs is wrong, mistaken, naive, misguided, bad or evil. Unexamined core beliefs keep us locked in society's paradigms, like those in Plato's cave who believed shadows were real, and attacked anyone who suggested there was freedom outside.

It is not the beliefs themselves (we all have them), but the attachment to them, or not examining them and seeing them as self-evident, that causes problems. Without being attached to core beliefs, we would much more readily see the world as it is, not how we think it should be. We would not feel threatened by those who do not share our views. Helping supervisees recognize some of their core beliefs enables them to work with a greater range of clients, to be less reactive or judgmental, not to oversimplify the issues. They begin to understand that the view about a situation, client, colleague or organization can be seen in many different ways. Paradoxically, by not being so attached, there is more space for change. In not being so sure that my world view is the correct or only one, I am less likely to polarize with those who disagree, less likely to try to impose change and meet resistance. I will start with a stance of inquiry.

Above, I stated a core belief about love being the essence of who we are. As with any belief, I will find the 'evidence' to support it. I keep this belief because I think it serves me, but I cannot be sure. There are many who would think that this core belief is plainly foolish given the wars, rapes, selfishness in the world. Yet, whether it is true or not (and it is unprovable) it informs most, if not all, of my work. I believe that when I or others act in a non-loving way, we must be afraid. This belief affects how I interact with them.

For example, continuing with the theme from the earlier dream, I see aggression as a form of fear. This has been a useful reframing for me when I experience myself attacking or being attacked. A moving example occurred when I was explaining this idea of aggression as a cover for fear to a supervision training group. One of the group had been asking for supervision on a young adult who was part of a home for those with severe handicaps. The young woman, whose case had been brought to supervision by the trainee, was sometimes so violent that it took four people to get her up in the morning. The trainee realized that it had never occurred to her or any of the staff that the young person was terrified. ('Wouldn't you be if you were suddenly awoken by someone and had three more people waiting outside the door?' she said, appalled at her own blind spot at not seeing this before.) She went back with this insight, approached the young person gently and slowly, explaining what she was wanting and why. Within two days, the previously violent young person was full of warmth and affection, asking for cuddles whenever she could. The supervisee reported this the following session, full of gratitude, hardly believing such a huge change was possible in such a short period of time.

Einstein considered the most important question of all was, 'Is the universe a friendly or an unfriendly place?' A core belief about a friendly universe is more likely to lead us to love; a core belief that it is unfriendly will lead us to fear.

Helping and helplessness

A challenging core belief for those in the helping professions might be 'I am responsible for my clients' welfare'. If we examine this belief, we can begin to see why carers sometimes lurch between feelings of impotence and omnipotence. The point is not to debate whether we are or aren't responsible for another, or to abdicate professional responsibility, but to see where the belief takes us. This one, for example, can lead us to an overprotectiveness, taking too much responsibility; or to a preoccupation with covering our backs for fear of being blamed; or to feeling a failure when we can't give the help we want, or when the help doesn't work. As a supervisor am I taking on too much responsibility or trying to find a solution to avoid feelings of helplessness, a possible parallel process stemming from the client? How would I know I was doing this? It could be so automatic, so spontaneous, so caring in society's terms. An even more challenging question. Can I ever really know what is useful for another, what truly helps? (For a much fuller discussion of staying with helplessness see Jochen Encke's description of his work with asylum seekers in Chapter 1.) Are we willing to go to the heart of this helping process, uncovering layer after layer of assumptions about our roles? Can we stay inquiring when action seems to be required?

Safe uncertainty and taking risks

In attaching to core beliefs we try to make the world fit our belief systems. Supervision can offer us a place to watch how we might present material in a particular way to fit in with our pictures of the world, or reveal an attachment to a particular outcome. We decide that in an uncertain world, certain things are the way the world is, or should be. (A good way of accessing core beliefs is via 'shoulds'.) The beliefs offer us a haven, a sense of certainty, but at great cost. In selecting the evidence to fit our beliefs, we can no longer be present to what is. We become unable to deal with the present moment. When Bion (2001) says we should enter the consulting room without Memory, Desire or Understanding, he is asking us to be present, not holding on to the past, not wanting a particular outcome, and not trying to make premature sense. He is asking us to dare to leap into the unknown.

In a paper called 'Towards positions of safe uncertainty', the author Barry Mason (1993) writes that to rush to a state of certainty, of knowing, is to avoid a sense of anxiety about not knowing, when not knowing is the most useful therapeutic response. Safe certainty says that the safety is in the solutions, the answers. There is a right way, and if it is not followed, then someone will be to blame. Safe uncertainty says that being comfortable with not knowing allows more scope for creativity, to see what this particular person at this particular time might need.

Safe uncertainty is similar to not knowing which forms the basis of most, if not all, spiritual traditions. Michael Carroll has written a chapter called the Spirituality of Supervision in which he distinguishes between religious supervision and spiritual supervision (Carroll 2001). The former asks for certainty, knowledge, outcomes, a way of keeping us imprisoned. The latter values not knowing. I think De Mello is saying the same thing when he says:

> Obedience keeps the rules. Love knows when to break them.
> (De Mello 1985)

In a therapeutic community where I was the group supervisor, someone was accused (wrongly as everyone in the group intuitively knew) of malpractice and suspended. Her colleagues were very worried about her as they had heard she was very depressed. I asked them if they were in contact and they looked at me as if I were from another planet. 'It's not allowed,' they said. I asked why. 'Because it's policy,' was the answer. I said I was baffled. There might have been instances where that was appropriate, but was this one of them? They were shocked at how they had let a rule overcome their natural compassion. As a supervisor, I was outside their belief system, and so could question their adherence to the rules.

We supervise (and write!) who we are: embracing paradox

Michael Carroll (2001) distinguishes between functional supervision – supervision as technology, and a philosophy of supervision – supervision as a way of being. The latter happens when work changes from just being a job, or indeed even a career, to becoming an extension of who we are. He writes:

> Is it possible that a supervisory attitude, viewing supervision as a reflective process that allows participants to think deeply and vulnerably about life and values, work and career, relationship and connections, might make an immense difference in how participants live? (Carroll 2001, p.77)

I see my job as creating a safe enough container in supervision for this to happen. Beyond that, adopting what Carroll calls the 'supervisory attitude' is my passion. As he says, it extends into a way of life, who we are, and acknowledging our interconnectedness.

It is easy to avoid concentrating on who we are and focus on theory, technique, schools of therapy. The question 'Who am I?' challenges so many of our core beliefs. We build up our identities and hold on to them, and anything we hold on to, we must by definition fear losing. When I get past I am a man, a father, a son, a therapist, a supervisor, a friend, writer, partner, past such descriptions such as I am generous, kind, cruel, lazy, what is left? I am faced with the paradox that only extreme crises have shown a self beyond the personality known as Robin, and I do everything in my power to avoid these crises. I saw this very clearly when, in a moment of insight with a spiritual teacher, I realized that everything, but everything, I did was to keep the image of Robin alive. And while doing this, I could not but be frightened. I saw that the image of Robin was not true, a story, and my protecting something not true was bound to create fear.

Fear is happening as I write and may be happening as you read. Can I be vulnerable with you when I do not even know how much I am hiding? The spiritual teacher mentioned above said, 'Personalities don't love. They want something' and encouraged us to ask who we would be without our personalities, our stories of who we think we are. The young nine-year-old girl Anna in the marvellous book *Mister God. This is Anna* put it simply, 'When you fink you are, you aint.'

The prospect of losing our identities, our beliefs about who think we are can fill us with fear:

> Come to the edge Life said.
> They said: We are afraid.
> Come to the edge Life said.
> They came. It pushed them…
> And they flew. (Guillaume Apollinaire, 1971)

I hear that voice, peer nervously over the edge, stubbornly tell Life no-one pushes me around, write about the fear of flying and eventually jump. That voice omitted to say that it had to be done again and again and it never became easier.

In a group supervision in a hospital, as the supervisees were describing their practices, I blurted out 'You are all frauds.' There was a shocked, but thoughtful silence for a few moments in which I tried to self-supervise why I had said that. It could have sounded very condemning, but I knew I did not feel like that towards the group. In fact I felt very supportive and thought they were working in an almost impossible situation. I waited to see what would happen, trusting that however it sounded they would hear the support in my challenge. 'Yes,' said one. 'I pretend to know things when I don't.' I didn't want to rescue too early, but thought it was time to share that that statement obviously included me. One by one we started to share where we were not congruent in our work. At that moment we became congruent, illustrating the beauty and challenge of paradox. When we take up one position, another becomes true. The following story invites us into a both/and position, rather than an either/or.

Two men were having an argument. One of them went to the wise village elder and told his side of the story. The elder said, 'You are right.' The second man heard this and indignantly went to see the elder. On hearing his story the elder said, 'You are right.' The elder's son said in a puzzled tone, 'They are saying opposite things. Both can't be right.' Whereupon the elder said to his son, 'You are right.'

I remember a conversation with a minister friend of mine who was stuck about what to deliver his sermon on, and asked me what I thought was the nature of God. I spontaneously replied, 'Love, Humour and Paradox.' Good ingredients for supervision, too.

Tracking fear

The essence of this chapter is that the purpose of focusing on fear is to replace distance and alienation with connection. A supervisee said, 'I think you use fear if it leads to love. I've often in your company faced fear I didn't know I had.'

As the supervisee alluded to, fear can take many forms that we may not recognize as fear. Even as I write at the time of the

World Cup, the footballers are celebrating madly when a goal is scored. It looks like joy, but feels like relief to me. As a friend put it:

> They are all driven by fear of losing, the fear of being judged, fear of the press, fear of losing their status, fear of being not good enough, failing – and when they score a goal, all that screaming and going wild and hugging is just a relief [from that fear] – but it all stays in the realm of fear.

The supervisees in the therapeutic community described in an earlier section were following procedures that went against their natural instincts, and did not realize how much they had become part of a prevalent culture of fear. Years later, on seeing one of them again, we laughed together as we recalled how furious she had been for my daring to question her behaviour, and what a relief it had been when she saw what she had been doing.

Evidence of the prevalence of fear in one to one sessions comes from the work of Kagan (1980) and using video playback (IPR – interpersonal process recall). He found that people perceive and understand much more of their communication with each other than one would suspect as one observes the interaction: the problem was that they were afraid to act on their perceptions. Through the IPR the students were helped to face their fears and practice skills that helped them be more present. His evidence supports the hypothesis that fear is the biggest block to intimacy and communication. In supervision it can lead to both supervisor and supervisee playing power games. These have been well and amusingly described by Hawthorne (1975) and Kadushin (1968).

A close relation to fear is shame which like fear can be hard to spot and stop us connecting and learning. We expect the supervisory relationship to be more adult than the therapeutic one so when primitive feelings are evoked, we can feel ashamed to bring them up. There can also be an evaluative aspect to supervision – both real and imagined, evoking previous images from school and parental situations.

Naming fear

Here are three examples from training and group supervision to illustrate how naming a fear moved us on.

I am running a day's training for clinical psychologists. It is the morning break and one of them suggests we go to her department for coffee as it is much nicer than the place we have been allocated. After the break she does not appear for 20 minutes. I ask her why and she says there was an emergency. I say I am puzzled. If we had not gone back to her department she would not have known about it, so how could it be an emergency? She shares that a staff member was suicidal and she had to check to see if the staff member was OK. I keep going. 'I do not understand,' I say. 'If we hadn't had the tea break at your department, you would have found out at the end of the day, so why was it an emergency?' I am seen as very uncaring by her, and increasingly the group. It also looks as if I am rigid about time boundaries and am punishing her. I ask her for the thought before she decided not to come back. A pause. Then tears. 'Once people knew that I knew, I had to do something.' 'Why?' I ask. 'Because last time I didn't phone immediately and she made a suicide attempt. If I had phoned we would have known earlier.' She and the group see how her checking on the staff member was not caring, but a form of protection, a fear response. A very understandable, but unconscious one. There is great compassion in the room where before there had been anger. We understand, and share examples of where we have covered our backs.

A second example. I am called into work with a group of middle managers in a college of further education where there are going to be redundancies. There is tension in the group, with some seen as 'favourites' for the chop. Everyone is very guarded, not wanting to reveal anything that could be seen as weakness, and give ammunition that could jeopardize their cause. I suggest that there is no way everyone could not be frightened. They were in a situation where there were going to be winners and losers and the stakes were high. I guess that it was not a safe situation. There were nods. I suggest that we all look at our responses to fear. For example, I withdraw, blame, intellectualize or get clever/smart arse. Some people go into workaholism, need to control, get cynical, procrastinate, or gossip and create cliques. We start to share our strategies and there are smiles as the group recognize each others' strategies. Compassion enters the room to replace the fear. Colleagues whose behaviour had been seen as impossible are now seen in a different light, understood as a response to fear. The outcome is that they decide to act as one body and take pay cuts if necessary to keep everyone on.

As I write, I am completing a supervisor training in Belfast. There have been magical moments, but I have an anxiety, an uncertainty. I have not reached the point where I can trust the process, where I believe love can hold us. I am still being skilful rather than being totally open. How easy it is to hide behind my expertise. I wonder why I am doing this as I like the individuals and the group. I have supervision and realize that I am holding back from mentioning the Troubles – the elephant in the room. I rationalize that it's not my job, that I am an outsider. But I realize my holding back is a fear response that is blocking intimacy. Behind the quick humour, theirs and mine, is an unease. Will I have the courage? However, in the next session a group member from Southern Ireland takes the risk. She is shaking and fears she will be attacked for mentioning it. Some of the group are angry – why does this always have to come up – but others are relieved and grateful. All appreciate her courage and the group feels safer. The quick humour is replaced by thoughtfulness and more measured interventions.

A system and a supervisee protecting themselves

Some time ago (around 2000) there was a Channel 4 Programme called 'Why Doctors Make Mistakes'. What was discovered is that when hospitals were open about mistakes and had a full inquiry, the litigation rates went down. Patients felt heard and were able to accept that mistakes happen. Far from making matters worse, accepting responsibility benefited the patients, the doctors and the hospitals. The system was able to learn from its mistakes, and changes in procedure put in place. When there was denial the system was using its energy to protect itself.

Another example from supervision, this time from Bruno Bettelheim (1993). He is supervising a student who starts his session with, 'I want to talk about a boy who is destroying the environment.' Bettelheim challenges him with irony by saying, 'A boy has difficulty in destroying the environment single handedly. If I didn't know better I would think you were trying to prejudice me against this boy.'

The point behind this is that if I am frightened, to justify my fear, I make the situation terrifying. I can't handle this boy, so I make him into an ogre. This way of justifying fear by making the other all powerful and destructive can justify going to war or trying to eliminate a whole race, tribe or religion.

Taking the 'supervisory attitude'

Here is a story, outside of supervision, of how imagining a catastrophic story could have created fear. It is an instance when I did not take the fear route; when, in fact, I took the 'supervisory attitude' mentioned earlier. I have a camper van and the day before I had had a tyre changed. The next day I am driving and I hear a rattling. A moment later I watch the whole wheel roll along the road and I am on three wheels. Obviously the bolts had not been put on properly the day before. Now it so happens that I was only going at ten miles an hour, as I was turning a corner; it is on a one-way road with not much traffic, quite visible, with plenty of room to pass. I have no-one with me and I am not in a hurry. I am quite calm as I ring the garage who get very defensive. However, I am not blaming, but just say I cannot put the wheel back myself and would really appreciate their help. The job gets done and I marvel at how I did not tell a fear story – I could have had my children with me, I could have been speeding on a motorway, the van could have tipped over, etc. Fear about what could have happened would have led to attacking the garage, who would never have come to put the wheel back on for fear of being – yes you got it – sued. People say, 'But it could have been terrible' and I can only say, 'But it wasn't.' The fear that leads us to imagine bad scenarios in this instance would not have been useful.

I am not usually so present in my ability to respond in the outside world. I value supervision so much because it offers a space, a structure, a meeting, that enables me to slow down my habitual responses and choose more awarely ones that might serve all parties. It is both part of life and a practice for life. When I do not jump to conclusions, I can take the opportunity to inquire, be curious, move towards a position of safe uncertainty.

In attempting to make the world a place of safe certainty, trying to avoid risk, we reinforce fear. Why defend if there isn't attack? So the defence becomes the attack, getting our retaliation in first. I wonder if fear itself is running the show, and we have become adept at rationalizing, explaining and denying it. I am not talking about fear of immediate danger, say when a lion is approaching. The fear I am talking about is conditioned fear, imagining fearful futures, believing other people's stories, not trusting our own experiences, our intuition, because others know better.

Mulla Nasruddin was ringing bells and banging a drum in his garden in the middle of London. A follower asked why he was doing this and he replied, 'To keep away the wolves.' 'But,' said the follower, 'there aren't any wolves in London.' To which Mulla Nasruddin replied, 'See, it's working.' We take measures to keep away danger when there might actually be no danger or when the danger has long passed. The wolves are in our minds.

What are you afraid to tell?

The founder of Non-Violent Communication (NVC), Marshall Rosenberg (2001), says that when he works with couples a very useful question is for each party to ask, 'What are you afraid to tell me?' This is the area the couple needs to go into to move their relationship on. I used a version of this question with a woman who was separating from her husband and unsure whether she was doing the right thing. 'What haven't you told him?' I asked. 'That I am infatuated with someone else,' she said. 'And you haven't told him because…' 'Because I am afraid of his reaction.' 'Which will be?' 'Anger.' 'And then what happens?' Gradually she realized that she needed to be open and risk the consequences. Her husband was then able to be more open with her, and although they separated it was done in a way that was more truthful and honest.

I sometimes start my training with asking people to write what they would least like people to know about their work. There is much reticence, mitigated by my promising that they would not have to share what they have written. I then ask them to finish the sentence, 'I don't want people to know about this because...' This time I ask them to share their reasons. The reasons cluster around shame, fear of being judged, feeling a fraud, not being good enough. These reasons are easier to share than the content of what they don't want people to know. However, when we examine these reasons, they often turn out to be unjustified. Participants make comments like 'I don't really think people will judge,' or 'I am the one who is judging.' Often they share what a few minutes ago they would never have believed they would. We realize how much energy is locked in fear.

Bringing it out

Cheri Huber (1995) in her book called *The Fear Book* writes that fear has a life of its own. It masquerades as a form of protection urging us to take precautions. These sound plausible until we don't do what fear wants. It then turns very nasty and it is shown to be not a protector at all, but a parasite which has found a very comfortable existence in us. She encourages us to examine every fear, not to conquer them, but to understand the process of how fear works.

Here are some questions which you may find useful to reflect on:

- Would you be willing to talk about fear in your sessions, either as supervisor or supervisee?

- If not, what is holding you back?

- What are you finding it difficult to say?

- What areas like power, authority, sexuality, race, gender might you be avoiding?

- Do you gossip at all about the other?

- As supervisor do you find yourself telling, advising, judging?

- If you hold the possibility that these may sometimes be fear responses, what fear are these interventions hiding?

- Are there monkeys on your back?

- If so what are they urging you to do or not do?

- If you thought of yourself as a passionate supervisor would you make different interventions?

- Would your style be different?

- How?

- As a supervisee do you find yourself wanting to please, editing, unable to say what you want?

- Could this be a response to fear and if so what is the fear?

- Often, especially on training courses, fears centre around assessment. Can you bring this to supervision?

- Did you know that supervisors may be equally as frightened by the assessment process?

- What strategies for facing fear have you found useful in the past?

- Can they help now?

- Would you present differently if you thought of yourself as a passionate supervisee?

- If you were to take a risk, what would it be?

I have mentioned strategies, but in fact any strategy that is not done with an open heart, will fail. 'Don't therapy me, NVC me, social work me' are comments that I have heard. One of the best ways of dealing with fear is an open heart. The reason why I have focused on fear is that it blocks an open heart.

Recognizing fear, naming it and sharing it are all ways of going beyond it. And there are very few people who do not enjoy the experience of being open-hearted. But fear comes in. 'I was caught being open, never again. My last supervisee took out a complaint. I have now got a three page contract.' The fear will find a crack in that contract, an ambiguity, a situation not thought of. We cannot protect ourselves by building walls (fear), but by staying open.

Opening our hearts

In Louise Erdrich's (2006) novel, *Four Souls*, she has one of the characters say 'So you see, once a person drops the scales of prejudiced certainty and doubts appear, there is no telling how far a heart can open' (p.98). This chapter has been about dropping the scales of prejudiced certainty which are driven by fear, welcoming doubt, and opening our hearts.

A moment. I am seeing an alternative health practitioner about trouble with my teeth. We are overrunning and she sees me anxious, because I know someone is in her waiting room. 'It's my job to take care of the session, not yours,' she says. I am very relieved that she has spotted a pattern of mine. The following week she is late and consequently my session overruns again, but this time I am late for my work. It is some consultancy work I have been doing for nine years and the only time I have been late. The group is quite challenging of me, and I struggle not to be defensive. When I see my health practitioner again, I reproach her for not taking care of the boundaries as she promised. She pauses and says, 'I want to apologize to your soul. I did not keep my word.' A great sense of well-being floods me and I say, 'My soul does not need you to apologize. It is fine and always has been. And it is full of gladness that you have.' In that moment both our hearts open, and a blame situation turns into a loving moment as she does not defend. Carroll quotes a theologian who says that God exists between people. In that moment of connectedness it was as if God came into the room.

Sheila Ryan says it in a different way, but I believe is essentially saying the same thing:

> The heart is Ariadne's thread leading the way home… Without engaging the heart, we journey hither and thither and find no resting place. (Personal communication)

As a way of engaging the heart, I have been using appreciative inquiry. This method asks people to focus on what is working well, what they appreciate, what gives them life. I have used it in schools, but my most moving experience came from a family of a husband and a third wife and her stepdaughter – the husband's daughter. As part of the process the stepmother asked her stepdaughter what she appreciated about the family. The reply was, 'Nothing, it is all crap.' I realized I had made a mistake and switched roles so that the daughter was asking her stepmother what she appreciated in the family. Her answers included some very positive comments about her stepdaughter which took the latter by surprise. We switched roles and one of the questions the stepmother asked her stepdaughter was 'What do you appreciate about me?' The previously hostile daughter said with real warmth and gratitude, 'You are the first person who has made my dad happy.' At that moment the teenager opened all our hearts.

Finally, many years ago I was involved in organizing a conference on accreditation. We wanted to find a form that would enable all parties to be on the same side, rather than one party judging another often not even face-to-face where there was little opportunity for relationship. I suggested people talked about what they loved in their work, what was important to them, a moment of gladness and appreciation that they were doing what they were doing. One by one people talked in front of the group. Apart from being a very moving experience, participants said they had lost their fear of being judged by an accreditation process. They had something inside themselves which could not be taken away by any external process. This something, I believe is love.

References

Apollinaire, G. (1971) *Selected Writings.* New York: New Direction Books.

Bettelheim, B. and Rosenfield, A. (1993) *The Art of the Obvious.* London: Thames and Hudson.

Bion, W.R. (2001) *Attention and Interpretation.* London: Routledge.

Carroll, M. (2001) 'The spirituality of supervision.' In M. Carroll and M. Tholstrup (eds) *Integrative Approaches to Supervision.* London: Jessica Kingsley Publishers.

De Mello, A. (1985) *One Minute Wisdom.* Anand, India: Guiarat Sahitya Prakash.

Erdrich, L. (2006) *Four Souls.* London: Harper Perennial.

Fynn (1974) *Mister God. This is Anna.* London: Collins.

Hawthorne, L. (1975) 'Games supervisors play.' *Social Work 20,* 3, 179–183.

Huber, C. (1995) *The Fear Book.* Murphys, CA: Keep it Simple Books.

Kadushin, A. (1968) *Supervision in Social Work,* 3rd edition. New York: Columbia University Press.

Kagan, N. (1980) 'Influencing human interaction – Eighteen years with IPR.' In A.K. Hess (ed.) *Psychotherapy Supervision: Theory, Research and Practice.* New York: Wiley.

Mason, B. (1993) 'Towards positions of safe uncertainty.' *Journal of Family Therapy 27,* 3, 298–301.

Rosenberg, M. (2001) *Nonviolent Communication.* Del Mar, CA: Puddle Dancer Press.

The Contributors

Anna Chesner is a Senior Trainer at the London Centre for Psychodrama Group and Individual Psychotherapy, and practises in London as a creative psychotherapist. She is an active member of the British Psychodrama Association, and is a passionate founder member of Playback AME Theatre company.

Jochen Encke has been living and working with his partner Ulrike in London for more than 25 years. They have two grown-up children. He finds that his formal education and trainings have done little in comparison to what his clients, family and friends (not necessarily always in this order) have taught him. The chapter here draws from these experiences and brings together what he feels has made him into what he is today.

Julie Hewson has been an educator in one form or another most of her life. She has been a teacher, lecturer, community education pioneer as well as founder of the Iron Mill Institute, and the Czech Institute of Supervision. She is a painter, potter, gardener and singer and an avid reader of stories from all over the world.

David Owen did his medical training in London. For 25 years he has worked as a homeopathic physician, working closely with other therapists. Supervision has been an invaluable tool in developing his personal and professional awareness. David is passionate about supervision as a process for allowing deep and therapeutic communication between therapist and client.

He has written about his transition from conventional medicine to homeopathy in *Passionate Medicine*. He has also recently completed a book on the principles and practice of homeopathy that describes different models of health and approaches to treatment that homeopaths can use. In addition to running his practice he is a senior clinical teaching fellow at Southampton Medical School (UK) where he teaches on holism.

Jane Reed is a coach, consultant and university lecturer working mainly in education settings. She is currently the part-time head of the International School Improvement Centre at the London Centre for Leadership in Learning at The Institute of Education, London University. The network supports schools that are developing their learning-centred practices across the country with publications and events. She is also a member of The Findhorn Foundation College Board and an Associate of the Nowhere Foundation. She co-wrote *The Intelligent School* with Barbara Macgilchrist and Kate Myers.

Sheila Ryan is a Fellow of the Society of Homeopaths. Her consultancy Sea Change supports practitioners, teams and organizations with supervision here and abroad. She is Clinical Practice Director at the School of Homeopathy and co-facilitates the Iron Mill Supervision Diploma. She is a founder member of the Ghana homeopathy project and author of *Vital Practice*, a homeopathic approach to supervision. Sheila lives on the Isle of Portland in Dorset with her husband and son. info@seachangeuk.com

Robin Shohet has been teaching supervision for 28 years through the Centre for Supervision and Team Development (www.cstd.co.uk). He is co-author with Peter Hawkins of

Supervision in the Helping Profession (OU Press, 3rd edition, 2006). His spiritual teachers have been his family, *A Course in Miracles* and Byron Katie (www.thework.org). He has recently developed an interest in equine therapy which he is bringing to his supervision practice. He lives at the Findhorn Foundation, a spiritual community in North East Scotland.

Joan Wilmot has been working as a psychotherapist and supervisor for 35 years. Two of her role models are Carol Jefferies, a Jungian therapist and Winifred Rushforth, an analyst, both of whom worked well into their nineties. She is a mother to four sons who, along with her partner, all love her and tease her outrageously, an associate member of the Findhorn community, member of Findhorn Playback theatre and co-writer of *The Boxing Clever Cookbook* with her good friend Jacqui Jones.

Joe Wilmot is an educational youth worker in central London. He works with young people who are at risk of being, or who have been, excluded from school. Joe has been working as a supervisor for the last three years, and in particular he supervises youth work students within his borough. When not working Joe likes to eat fine food, attend the theatre and play saxophone in exchange for beer.

Lia Zografou, MA (University of Surrey, Roehampton) is a dramatherapist and supervisor who lives and works in Thessaloniki, Greece. She is also a trained actress, director and Playback theatre practitioner.

Subject Index

Author Index